D1162985

ADLAI E. STEVENSON HIGH SCHOOL
THE LIBRARY
ONE STEVENSON DRIVE
LINCOLNSHIRE, IL 60069

DATE DUE

DEMCO, INC. 38-2931

ADLAI E. STEVENSON HIGH SCHOOL
THE LIBRARY
ONE STEVENSON DRIVE
LINCOLNSHIRE, IL 60069

Furman v. Georgia:

DEBATING THE DEATH PENALTY

E UNDER LAW

SUPREME COURT MILESTONES

Furman v. Georgia:

DEBATING THE DEATH PENALTY

REBECCA STEFOFF

 **Marshall Cavendish**
Benchmark
New York

Marshall Cavendish Benchmark
99 White Plains Road
Tarrytown, NY 10591-9001
www.marshallcavendish.us

Library of Congress Cataloging-in-Publication Data
Stefoff, Rebecca [date]
Furman v. Georgia : debating the death penalty / by Rebecca Stefoff.
p. cm. — (Supreme Court milestones)
Includes bibliographical references and index.
ISBN 978-0-7614-2583-0
1. Furman, William Henry—Trials, litigation, etc.—Juvenile literature. 2. Georgia—
Trials, litigation, etc.—Juvenile literature. 3. Capital punishment—United States—
Juvenile literature. 4. Capital punishment—Georgia—Juvenile literature.
I. Title. II. Series.
KF228.F87S747 2007
345.73'0773—dc22
2007000582

Photo Research by Connie Gardner

Cover Photo by: Chris Kleponis/AFP/Getty

The photographs in this book are used by permission and through the courtesy of:
Corbis: Royalty-free, 2–3; Reuters, 13; Bettmann, 16, 37, 58, 82, 85, 105; Amy
Toensing, 108; *North Wind Picture Archive:* 20; *AP Photo:* 30, 46, 50, 111, 112; Morning
Sentinel, 24; *The Granger Collection:* 44; *Getty:* Time Life Pictures, 63, 67; New York
Times/Hulton, 78.

Publisher: Michelle Bisson
Art Director: Anahid Hamparian
Series Designer: Sonia Chaghatzbanian

Printed in China
1 3 5 6 4 2

contents

WILLIAM HENRY FURMAN AT THE TIME OF THE ARREST THAT WOULD PLACE HIM ON DEATH ROW.

one
"I JUST WANTED TO STAY ALIVE"

NINETY-NINE CONVICTS in a Florida prison watched the cop movie *Dirty Harry* on June 29, 1972. Just after the movie ended, a guard passed them a piece of news. The men reacted immediately. "We laughed, we whooped, we hollered and shook the doors," said a convict named Calvin Campbell. What news had caused this celebration? The men were on Death Row, sentenced to capital punishment for their crimes. And the U.S. Supreme Court, in one of the most controversial decisions of its history, had just handed down a ruling that would save their lives.

The death penalty, the Court had declared, was unconstitutional. As it was being applied in the United States at the time, it violated the Eighth Amendment of the U.S. Constitution, which bans "cruel and unusual punishments."

Six hundred and twenty-nine people were under sentence of death in prisons across the United States on that day. Each one of them was spared execution. A few of them received new trials. Most of them had their sentences changed to life in prison, although many were later released on parole. Years later, legal journalist Joan Cheever tracked down one of these released convicts, a man named William Henry Furman. He had been one of the six hundred and twenty-nine on Death Row that June day in 1972—and it was his case, *Furman* v. *Georgia*, that had made the Supreme Court throw out the death penalty.

Cheever asked Furman how he felt about ending the death penalty and saving all those lives.

Furman shrugged and seemed uncomfortable. "I didn't do nuthin' back then but try to stay alive," he said. "I just wanted to stay alive."

The Supreme Court's decision in *Furman* v. *Georgia* kicked off heated debates about capital punishment. On one side were people who believed that execution by the state was wrong and should never occur again. On the other were people who believed that death was the proper punishment for heinous crimes such as murder. The argument was not new; it had been going on for several hundred years. By the mid-twentieth century it had become entangled with questions of race and fairness, as well as morality and crime prevention.

Furman v. *Georgia*, the case that banned the death penalty, was only the most recent chapter in the long, tortuous story of capital punishment, and it wouldn't be the last. Within a few years, the death penalty would come roaring back into American life. By that time, William Henry Furman's role in the story would be over. His part had begun in the dark hours of the early morning on August 11, 1967, when he made a bad decision that led to a needless tragedy.

A KILLING IN SAVANNAH

Furman was intent on burglary when he walked up to a house in Savannah, Georgia, at about two o'clock that morning. Inside the house, William and Lanelle Micke and their five children were sleeping. Furman later said that he was drunk at the time.

On the rear porch of the Micke home, Furman

approached the back door. Next to the door was a window with a washing machine standing in front of it. Furman moved the washing machine so that he could open the window. Reaching in through the window, he opened the door from the inside and entered the house.

William Micke woke up and heard a noise in the kitchen. He thought the sound must have been made by one of his children, a boy who was prone to sleepwalking, and got up to take the child back to bed. Lanelle Micke later reported that she heard William go into the kitchen, and then she heard a loud sound followed by a scream from her husband. She brought the children into her bedroom and called the police. She and the children waited in the bedroom until they arrived.

The first officer on the scene found William Micke on the kitchen floor, surrounded by blood from a gunshot wound. He was dead. A second officer spotted a figure leaving a nearby patch of woods. The figure started running, leaving tracks in the mud. The officer followed the tracks to a house not far away. In the crawl space under that house was William Henry Furman.

When the police pulled Furman out and searched him, they found a gun and arrested him. The gun proved to be the one that had fired the shot that killed William Micke, and Furman's fingerprints were found on the washing machine that had been moved on the Mickes' rear porch. The case seemed open-and-shut. The state of Georgia charged Furman with murder. Under Georgia law, if he were found guilty, he could receive the death penalty.

on trial for murder

Because Furman could not afford to hire a lawyer, he was granted a public defender—a defense attorney appointed by the court. That attorney was B. Clarence Mayfield. As the first step in building a case for the defense, Mayfield had Furman evaluated by the staff at a psychiatric hospital. If Furman were judged insane, Mayfield could enter an insanity plea.

Under the law, insanity as a criminal defense means that the defendant did not know right from wrong at the time of the crime and is not capable of assisting in his or her own defense. The insanity defense is rarely used, and when it is used, it is rarely successful. A study published in 2003 found that fewer than one percent of defendants facing felony charges tried the insanity defense. It was successful in about two cases of every thousand. In Furman's case, the evaluation produced by the super-intendent of the hospital failed to support an insanity plea for Mayfield's client. The superintendent reported that, "[Furman] is not psychotic at present, knows right from wrong and is able to cooperate with his counsel in preparing his defense."

Furman's trial for the murder of William Micke took place in superior court in Chatham County, Georgia, on September 28, 1968. The prosecutor, the attorney acting on behalf of the state, presented evidence that Furman had broken into the Micke house. The arresting officer said that Furman had told him that when William Micke entered the kitchen, Furman went out through the back door. The door closed behind him. As Furman left the scene, he turned and fired a shot at the house. That bullet passed through the plywood door and killed William Micke.

When Furman took the stand in his own defense, he did not dispute the prosecution's claim that he had broken into the Micke house, or that William Micke had surprised him. His account of the shooting, though, differed from the version that the officer said Furman had given at the time. Furman testified:

They got me charged with murder and I admit, I
admit going to these folks' home and they did
caught me in there and I was coming back out,
backing up and there was a wire down there on the
floor. I was coming out backwards and fell back
and I didn't intend to kill nobody. I didn't know
they was behind the door. The gun went off and I
didn't know nothing about no murder until they
arrested me, and when the gun went off I was down
on the floor and I got up and ran. That's all to it.

According to Furman's version of events, he didn't
turn and fire at the door. He fell, the gun went off accidentally, and he got up and ran away.

Furman's trial had started at about 10 o'clock in the
morning. By the middle of the afternoon, the defense and
the prosecution had finished their arguments. Now it was
up to the jury—and to Judge Dunbar Harrison, who gave the
jurors their instructions. Harrison's first important point
to the jurors was to clarify the meaning of "murder."
Georgia law defined murder as killing someone with *malice
aforethought*. This means that the murderer had the intention to do harm. Malice aforethought could be express, or
clear, as in the case of a planned, premeditated murder.
However, malice could also be implied, or indirect. The use
of a gun or any other deadly weapon in any killing implied
malice, because it meant that the person who wielded the
weapon had been prepared to act with deadly force.

Harrison also explained to the jurors the legal impact
of a killing that takes place during the course of another
crime, such as a burglary. If someone sets out to commit a
lesser crime, but kills another person as a consequence of
committing that crime, even by accident, the killing is a
type of homicide called *felony murder*.

Finally, Harrison told the jurors that they might be

required to make two decisions. First, they had to decide whether Furman was guilty or innocent of murder. If they found him guilty, they would also have to decide on his punishment. Under Georgia law, they would have two choices: life in prison, or death in the electric chair. They did not have to give the reasons for their choice, and their choice would be binding—in other words, the court would not overrule it.

After thirty-five minutes of deliberation, the jurors asked Judge Harrison whether they could limit their decision to the question of guilt or innocence and leave the question of punishment up to the court. He replied that state law made the jury responsible for both decisions. The jurors returned to their deliberations.

It took one more hour for the jury to reach its verdict. The jurors found Furman guilty of murder and recommended a sentence of death. Furman's execution was scheduled for November 8, 1969.

LAST CHANCE

Mayfield used the time between Furman's trial and his scheduled execution to try to save his client. His first step was to file a motion with Judge Harrison, asking for a retrial. Mayfield claimed that the first trial should not be allowed to stand because the prosecution had presented the jury with a confession that had been improperly obtained by the police. Furman's constitutional rights, Mayfield claimed, had been violated. Furman had not been properly "mirandized."

Today the term "mirandized" is familiar to the audiences of crime dramas, but in 1967, when Furman was arrested, it was new. It came from a 1966 U.S. Supreme Court decision called *Miranda v. Arizona*, involving a man named Ernesto Miranda who had been convicted of kidnapping and rape. One factor in Miranda's conviction was

THE DEATH PENALTY AROUSES FIERCE EMOTIONS. ON JUNE 10, 2001, ANTI-
DEATH PENALTY DEMONSTRATORS IN TERRE HAUTE, INDIANA, PROTESTED THE
EXECUTION OF OKLAHOMA CITY BOMBER TIMOTHY MCVEIGH. THE PROTESTS
DID NOT STOP HIS EXECUTION.

a confession he had made to the police. But the police officers stated at Miranda's trial that they had not told
Miranda that he had certain rights under the law—rights
that might have kept him from making that confession.

13

Those rights stem from the U.S. Constitution's Fifth Amendment, which states that no person "shall be compelled in any criminal case to be a witness against himself." This has been interpreted to mean that people can refuse to answer questions if the answers might incriminate them or might be used against them.

Attorneys for Miranda appealed the case to the Supreme Court, arguing that Miranda's confession should be thrown out. His conviction was not valid, they claimed, because he had not been informed of his legal rights. The Court agreed and overturned Miranda's rape conviction. It also ruled that anyone who is questioned by the police in connection with a crime must first be informed of three things: first, the subject has the right to remain silent; second, if the subject does say anything, it may be used against him or her in court; and third, the subject has the right to an attorney, and if he or she cannot afford one, the court will appoint a public defender.

After the Court's ruling in *Miranda*, police officers nationwide were ordered to read their rights to all suspects before questioning them, and this became known as mirandizing. In the case of William Henry Furman, a police detective had testified during the trial that Furman *had* been mirandized, but that he had waived his rights, or chosen to ignore them. Based on this testimony, Judge Harrison rejected Mayfield's claim that Furman's Fifth Amendment rights had been violated.

In Mayfield's motion for a new trial, however, the attorney also pointed to the Fourteenth Amendment to the Constitution. This amendment guarantees that all citizens are entitled to due process of law, and the courts had interpreted it to mean that the law is to be applied to all citizens equally and in the same manner. Mayfield pointed out in his motion that Georgia's state laws prevented trial judges from giving juries in capital trials any guidelines on how and when to choose the death penalty. Jurors had complete freedom to apply the death penalty—or not—as they chose. This meant that the death penalty was applied unevenly. The same crime, under the same circumstances, might bring execution in one case and life in prison in another, depending upon how the jury felt in each case. This fact, Mayfield claimed, had violated Furman's due-process rights, because it was not a consistent application of the law. Judge Harrison rejected this argument, too, on the grounds that Furman's sentence had been delivered in accordance with the state laws of Georgia.

With the motion for a retrial denied, Furman's attorney took the next step and appealed the case to a higher court, the Georgia Supreme Court. He prepared a brief, or statement of his arguments, for the court. Like Mayfield's earlier motion for a retrial, the brief rested on questions of constitutional rights.

In the brief, Mayfield again raised the issue of mirandizing. He claimed that Furman's Fifth Amendment rights had been violated because the police had questioned him about the shooting without reading him his rights. He also focused on the Sixth Amendment, which guarantees the right to be tried by "an impartial jury of the State." One potential juror in Furman's trial, Mayfield said, had been kept off the jury because he said that he had doubts about the use of the death penalty. Yet the U.S. Supreme Court had just decided, in a case called *Witherspoon* v. *Illinois*, that doubts about the death penalty could not be used to disqualify people from serving on the jury in a capital trial. If the only people who could serve on juries were those who had no doubts about capital punishment, the result would be juries slanted in favor of the death penalty. Such "hanging juries" would violate the Sixth Amendment. Only a juror who indicated utter refusal to use the death

THOSE WHO ARE IN FAVOR OF THE DEATH PENALTY ARE OFTEN VEHEMENT. IN 1986, PRO-DEATH PENALTY ADVOCATES EXPRESS THEIR SUPPORT FOR THE EXECUTION OF JAMES TERRY ROACH, WHO WAS ELECTROCUTED FOR KILLING TWO SOUTH CAROLINA TEENAGERS.

penalty in any circumstances could be disqualified. The potential juror in Furman's trial, Mayfield argued, had not expressed such firm views, and therefore he had been improperly excluded.

Mayfield's third argument was addressed to the Eighth Amendment, the one that prohibits "cruel and unusual punishments." Mayfield tried to make the case that death *was* a cruel and unusual punishment. He did not employ the Fourteenth Amendment argument, the question of due process, as a major element in the brief.

The state supreme court responded to Mayfield's brief on April 24, 1969. Its two-page response addressed his major arguments.

As far as the Fifth Amendment was concerned, the court found that Furman's rights had not been violated when the police obtained his statement. Beyond that, the court pointed out, Furman had gone on to testify in court that he had fired the gun when he tripped over a wire. This admission of an accidental shooting was enough to qualify the crime as felony murder and to uphold the guilty verdict.

The court didn't buy Mayfield's Sixth Amendment argument, either. This was the argument that turned on the matter of the juror who was disqualified because of doubts about the death penalty. In the opinion of the court, the disqualified juror had shown that his views on capital punishment might influence his vote on whether Furman was guilty or innocent. Because the juror would not have been capable of making an unbiased determination of the defendant's guilt or innocence, the prosecutor had an appropriate reason to keep him off the jury.

What about "cruel and unusual punishments"? The state supreme court rejected Mayfield's argument. It ruled that the Georgia laws that permitted the death penalty did not violate the Eighth Amendment.

Mayfield—and Furman—had lost the appeal to the highest court in Georgia. The court, however, recognized that Mayfield's arguments had rested on the U.S. Constitution. It felt that the U.S. Supreme Court, which decides constitutional questions, might agree to hear those arguments. The state supreme court granted Furman a stay, or delay, of execution so that Mayfield could submit the case to the highest court in the land.

The U.S. Supreme Court case would not be concerned

with whether William Henry Furman was guilty of killing William Micke, or even whether Furman's Fifth Amendment rights had been respected with proper mirandizing. The issue would be whether the sentence Furman had received under Georgia law was allowable under the U.S. Constitution. In effect, the death penalty itself would be on trial.

Allies stepped forward to help Mayfield get Furman's case before the U.S. Supreme Court. In fact, the case became part of a larger strategy to attack the death penalty. Furman had committed his crime and received his sentence at a time when a battle over capital punishment was being fought in American courtrooms, with the Supreme Court at the center of the controversy. Questions about whether the death penalty is right or wrong, however, had been raised many times before.

TWO
THE DEATH PENALTY
COMES TO AMERICA

"ONLY 13 BOYS WERE IN SCHOOL today," a lawyer
named Henry Van Der Lyn wrote in his journal on March 19,
1833, after hearing his son's account of his school day.
"The rest had gone to see the execution." The boys who
skipped school that day had witnessed the hanging of a
man in Chenango County, New York. In the early nineteenth century, executions of criminals were held in
public, as they had been for centuries. They often drew
large crowds and were considered "an especially wholesome experience for children," according to law professor
Stuart Banner.

Today, executions are not treated as public spectacles,
and most people would not call them wholesome, instruc-
tive entertainment for the young. Feelings about the death
penalty have changed in the past two centuries. Like
Furman v. *Georgia*, such changes in public attitudes are
part of the ongoing evolution of a punishment that is as old
as history.

ANCIENT EXECUTIONS
The laws of Hammurabi, a king of Babylon in the eighteenth century BCE, are the oldest known legal code in
the world. The list of crimes and punishments shows that

THE DEATH PENALTY HAS BEEN EXERCISED SINCE ANCIENT TIMES. IN THIS ANTIQUE HAND-COLORED PRINT, ONE ASSYRIAN SOLDIER HOLDS THE DECAPITATED HEAD OF A MAN WHO HAD BEEN EXECUTED.

the ancient Babylonian state inflicted the death penalty for twenty-five different offenses. Although people today generally think of murder as the crime most likely to result in the death penalty, it wasn't one of the capital offenses in Hammurabi's code.

Executions undoubtedly took place long before written records began, but the oldest known record of a specific instance of capital punishment comes from Egypt in the sixteenth century BCE. A member of the nobility was accused of a crime involving magic. He was required to commit suicide. Although the method of death was not specified, it probably didn't involve an ax—the weapon that was commonly used to execute criminals who were not nobles.

The early Jews, on the other hand, administered capital punishment in a variety of ways, including stoning, hanging, beheading, crucifixion, throwing people from high rocks, and even sawing them in two. Execution was part of their code of religious law, as reflected in Exodus 21 of the Old Testament, which says that God named death as the punishment for murder, kidnapping, striking a parent, or cursing a parent.

Most ancient law codes, like modern ones, provided varying degrees of punishment, depending upon the crime. But in the Greek city-state of Athens in the seventh century BCE, a lawgiver named Draco simplified matters with a legal code that gave the same punishment for every crime. That punishment was death. The Draconian legal code is the source of the modern adjective "draconian," meaning severe, harsh, even cruel. An execution that took place in Athens several centuries after Draco's time became one of the most famous cases of capital punishment in ancient history. In 399 BCE, the state convicted the philosopher Socrates of corrupting the young with his unconventional ideas. He was forced to end his life by drinking hemlock, a poison.

When the Romans codified their laws, beginning around the fifth century BCE, they specified punishments that varied not just according to the crime but according to the criminal's social class: slave, free person, or noble. Offenses that brought the death penalty ranged from publishing an insulting song, making a disturbance inside the city of Rome during the night, or burning a stack of grain near a house, to theft, perjury, or murder. Methods of execution included drowning at sea, crucifixion, beating, burial alive, and impalement. Romans who killed their parents met a strange but effective form of the death penalty: being sunk in water in a sack that also contained a dog, a rooster, a poisonous snake, and an ape.

"Cruel and Unusual"

The staggering array of offenses that have been punishable by death in various times and places can be broken down into four general categories. Crimes against religion are defined by each religion, but often they include such things as witchcraft and heresy (holding beliefs that differ from the doctrines of the official church). Treason and espionage are examples of crimes against the state. Crimes against the person include murder, rape, kidnapping, and assault. Finally, there are crimes against property, such as theft and arson.

The death penalty was not always aimed simply at killing the person who had committed the offense. Often, especially in its more gruesome forms, execution was meant to be a terrifying public spectacle that would not only show justice being done but also stand as a warning to onlookers of the dreadful fate that awaited offenders. Yet attitudes toward punishment—and the laws governing punishment—changed over time. For example, when Constantine became emperor of the Romans in the fourth century CE, he put an end to crucifixion and other cruel methods of execution.

The ancient Romans had employed different methods of execution for different classes of people, and that custom lingered in Europe, where some forms of death came to be seen as "higher," or more honorable, than others. Knights and nobles could be beheaded, while common criminals were more likely to be hanged. Beheading was a swifter, and therefore less agonizing, death—in theory. In practice, botched and prolonged executions occurred with both methods. In France in the late eighteenth century, at the height of the French Revolution,

Joseph-Ignace Guillotin developed an improved, more humane version of a decapitation device that had been used in various parts of Europe since the thirteenth century. Known as the guillotine, the doctor's machine administered death through mechanical action rather than by the direct act of a headsman or a hangman. It was a step toward consistent, standardized capital punishment.

Britain's laws and practices regarding the death penalty would have the most profound and lasting influence on capital punishment in the United States. In particular, British approaches to deciding what was an appropriate punishment would shape the development of American death penalty laws and legal decisions, including *Furman*.

One approach to the question of appropriate punishment is summed up in the phrase "let the punishment fit the crime." This reflects the belief that there should be some equity between crime and punishment—in other words, the severity of the penalty should match the seriousness of the offense. An early expression of this concept was written into the Magna Carta, a charter reluctantly signed by King John in 1215 that required all citizens, including the king, to abide by the rule of law. The Magna Carta stated that fines issued as penalties for crimes should match the degree of the offense.

The concept of equity between crime and punishment went beyond the amount of fines. When extended to other forms of punishment, it meant that the traditionally severe penalties could be reduced for certain crimes, such as cursing, that were no longer generally considered to be worthy of death. But although the notion that the punishment should fit the crime had been planted in the law, it was slow to take hold. Meanwhile, the number of capital crimes under British law kept increasing. By the eighteenth century, more than two hundred offenses were

THE MAGNA CARTA, ISSUED BY KING JOHN OF ENGLAND IN 1215, STATED THAT
FINES SHOULD MATCH THE DEGREE OF THE OFFENSE.

punishable by death. Among these capital crimes were
cutting down a tree and stealing a rabbit.

Eighteenth-century juries were sometimes unwilling
to deliver a guilty verdict if they felt that the punishment
far outweighed the crime. Jurors would rather find a
defendant not guilty than subject him or her to a punishment that seemed wildly out of proportion. British lawmakers responded by making changes to bring penalties
into line with offenses. Legal reforms in the mid-nine-
teenth century would greatly reduce the number of crimes
that carried the death penalty.

The law had also begun to reflect another idea about
punishment: the belief that excessively cruel penalties
should not be permitted. Since ancient times, society's

official torturers and executioners had displayed ghastly inventiveness in the many ways they found to torment the human body and to take life. As late as 1531, for example, boiling to death—which sometimes took several hours—was permitted as a method of execution in Britain. Some of the more lingering and ghoulish forms of execution were abandoned after the English Bill of Rights became law in 1689. One of its clauses read: "Excessive bail ought not to be required, nor excessive fines imposed, nor cruel and unusual punishments inflicted." This was the first explicit use of the language that would save William Henry Furman and more than six hundred other American convicts from death nearly three centuries later.

The 1689 law against "cruel and unusual punishments" did not bring an end to the death penalty itself. No one at the time would seriously have considered such a thing. Loss of life continued to be seen as the appropriate punishment for a wide range of crimes. In fact, other than fines, banishment, and physical punishments such as flogging or mutilation, execution was the only punishment. Jails existed to hold people who were awaiting trial and punishment, but the practice of punishing convicted criminals by incarcerating them in prisons did not arise until the late eighteenth century. Until then, the death penalty was seen as the best way to accomplish what modern penologists, or scholars of punishment, have defined as three of the goals of legal penalties: retribution (punishing criminals for their crimes), incapacitation (preventing them from committing more crimes), and deterrence (creating an example that will discourage other people from becoming criminals).

Although the move was under way toward more standardized and humane methods of execution, such as hanging, some of the judicial punishments that remained in use after 1689 would be regarded as excessively cruel by most people today. Pressing, for example, involved gradually crushing someone with heavy stones, adding one stone at a time. Although pressing was chiefly used to encourage suspected criminals to confess, it was sometimes used to execute them as well. During the eighteenth century, however, society came to see judicial torture as unacceptable. Such punishments as pressing, burning, and drowning fell out of use as legal penalties. Still, with its wide range of capital offenses, England's criminal code at that time was the harshest in Europe.

American Executions

In 1607 the English established their first permanent North American settlement at Jamestown, Virginia. The next year they carried out their first execution. They hanged a man named George Kendall, who was accused of "spying for the Spanish."

The English adventurers, speculators, and settlers who founded the American colonies did so under English law. Yet the colonies also enjoyed some freedom to make their own internal laws, which is why criminal codes—and the use of the death penalty—varied from place to place in the thirteen colonies.

Four years after Kendall was hanged in Virginia, the colony's governor, Sir Thomas Dale, introduced a criminal code that carried the death penalty for such things as stealing grapes and trading with the Indians. Within seven years, though, Virginia had to relax its draconian criminal code somewhat, to keep from frightening off prospective settlers. From that time on, the southern colonies generally followed the criminal code that was in use in England at any given time. Because crimes against property—even trivial ones—were capital offenses in England, they also carried the death penalty in the southern colonies.

The northern colonies, at first, did not punish burglary,

robbery, and other property crimes with death (at least, not until the third offense). On the other hand, the religious origins of Massachusetts and some of the other northern colonies led to capital punishment for things that were considered moral crimes, such as witchcraft and any kind of sexual behavior outside of marriage. During the eighteenth century, the northern colonies gradually dropped the death penalty for moral crimes. At the same time, partly because of pressure from the British government, the northern colonies increased the number of property crimes that carried the death penalty. In Pennsylvania, for example, rape, highway robbery, arson, burglary, and other offenses became capital crimes in 1718. Before that, murder had been the only crime punishable by death in the colony for more than thirty years.

Race was entangled with capital punishment in the American colonies, where some capital laws applied specifically to blacks. In Virginia, it was a capital crime for a slave to prepare medicine or administer it; this law reflected white slave-owners' fears of being poisoned. In South Carolina a slave or free black could be hanged for encouraging another slave to run away, or for any injury to a white person, even the slightest bruise.

When the thirteen colonies went to war for independence from Great Britain, they adopted new state constitutions. Eight of those constitutions included prohibitions against "cruel and unusual punishments," using the language of the English Bill of Rights. After independence was won, and the thirteen former colonies had joined together to form the United States, they faced the task of drafting a constitution that would embody the principles of their new federal, or national, government, as well as its laws. The U.S. Constitution that was adopted in 1787 had no bill of rights, but that gap was later filled by the first ten amendments, or changes, to the Constitution. Adopted in 1791, these ten amendments became known as the American Bill of Rights.

The Eighth Amendment used language copied exactly from the English Bill of Rights: "Excessive bail ought not to be required, nor excessive fines imposed, nor cruel and unusual punishments inflicted." This language caused some concern when Congress debated the amendments, before they were added to the Constitution. William Smith, a representative from South Carolina, felt that the phrase "cruel and unusual punishments" was vague and unclear. Samuel Livermore of New Hampshire said the same thing. The wish to spare people from excessive punishment was humane, Livermore declared. He had no objection to humane feelings. But there seemed to be no clear meaning in the language of the Eighth Amendment, so he found it unnecessary.

Livermore was especially worried that the Eighth Amendment might be used to do away with the death penalty. He said to Congress: "It is sometimes necessary to hang a man, villains often deserve whipping, and perhaps having their ears cut off." Then he asked, "Are we in future to be prevented from inflicting these punishments because they are cruel?"

The representative from New Hampshire was right to fear that the Eighth Amendment would someday be used to attack the death penalty. *Furman v. Georgia* was just one of many cases that would test the legality of the death penalty by appealing to the Eighth Amendment. But even before the amendment became law in the United States, a debate had already begun about whether capital punishment should be abolished.

AN ABOLITION MOVEMENT BEGINS

In 1764 an Italian legal scholar named Cesare Beccaria published a small volume called *An Essay on Crimes and*

Punishments. Translated into English, French, and German, it became part of the literature of the Enlightenment, an intellectual and philosophical movement that called for reason, rather than tradition and custom, to be the foundation of social and political institutions. Enlightenment thinkers and writers turned a critical, examining eye on such things as marriage, government— and crime and punishment.

Beccaria argued that there was no reasonable basis for the state to deprive someone of life. Execution, he said, was "a war of a whole nation against a citizen, whose destruction they consider as necessary, or useful to the general good." In other words, society uses its collective power to execute individual criminals because it thinks their deaths are necessary or useful. If the death penalty could be shown to be neither necessary nor useful, Beccaria said, it should be abolished. In Beccaria's view, the only time an execution was necessary was when nothing short of the criminal's death could guarantee national security, which would surely be a rare case. As for usefulness, it seemed clear that the death penalty was not serving the purpose of deterring other people from committing crimes, because crimes continued to be committed. Beccaria thought that "the continued example of a man deprived of liberty" in prison would be a better deterrent to crime than the brief spectacle of an execution.

Copies of Beccaria's book were sold in the American colonies. Thomas Jefferson, George Washington, and John Adams all owned the book, and it appeared in several colonial newspapers. It was part of the wave of Enlightenment thought that helped mold ideas in the colonies and contributed to the Revolutionary War, the Declaration of Independence, and the U.S. Constitution. Beccaria's work also inspired debate about the death penalty in the colonies.

A GROUP OF CAUCASIANS LOOK AT THE DEAD BODY OF AFRICAN AMERICAN RUBIN STACY, LYNCHED ON JULY 19, 1935. STACY HAD BEEN ACCUSED OF ATTACKING A WHITE WOMAN BUT WAS SEIZED BY A MOB BEFORE HE COULD BE TRIED.

During and immediately after the Revolutionary period, some Americans began to express the view that the death penalty was morally wrong, socially and politically ineffective, or both. Members of the Society of Friends, or Quakers, opposed capital punishment on religious grounds, as a violation of the biblical commandment "Thou shalt not kill" and of Jesus's instruction to "Love thy neighbor."

As an alternative to capital punishment, the Quakers promoted imprisonment, with the idea that life in prison would offer the condemned criminal an opportunity to repent the crime and experience spiritual growth. This development recognized a fourth goal of punishment: rehabilitation (giving a criminal an opportunity to mend his or her ways). It was partly due to Quaker influence that some states built the first prisons for long-term incarceration in the 1780s. Imprisonment began to replace such forms of punishment as whipping and forced labor. As states gradually modified their criminal codes, imprisonment would replace capital punishment for some crimes, including arson and robbery.

One of the first American documents in the discussion of the death penalty was *An Enquiry How Far the Punishment of Death is Necessary in Pennsylvania*, published in 1793 by William Bradford, Pennsylvania's attorney general. Although Bradford favored capital punishment, he concluded that the death penalty made it harder for the state to convict the guilty in some cases because juries did not want to sentence people to death. This feeling was reflected in a wave of new laws throughout the 1790s that curbed capital punishment, abolishing it for certain classes of crimes. Five states, for example, limited capital punishment to cases of murder.

Benjamin Rush, a Pennsylvania physician and a signer of the Declaration of Independence, argued in 1797 that the death penalty should not be used even against murderers. In a published lecture titled "Considerations on the Injustice and Impolity of Punishing Murder by Death," Rush suggested that capital punishment should be entirely eliminated. Both reason and religion, he argued, were against it. Some legal historians today consider Rush the founder of the American movement to abolish capital punishment.

Those boys who skipped school in 1833 to see the hanging in Chenango County witnessed one of the last

DEATH PENALTY POETRY

Public executions in seventeenth- and eighteenth-century America were seen as occasions for making moral statements about the righteousness of punishment and the grim fate that awaited those who broke the law. Often these moral statements appeared in the form of poems, usually anonymous, that were spread about on broadsides, or printed sheets. Broadsides might be handed out (or sold) at the execution, or distributed before or after the fatal event. As legal historian Stuart Banner shows in *The Death Penalty: An American History*, poems written about executions captured various aspects of the experience.

A poem could express sympathy for the convict along with the belief that the death sentence was fair. When Ebenezer Mason was hanged for killing his brother-in-law, one poet declared:

> Mason, alas! We mourn for you;
> Sentenc'd to die, as murderers do.

The execution of Ebenezer Ball, another murderer, produced these lines:

> But though we pity this poor BALL,
> Which we all do, I trust,
> Yet when we know for what he dy'd,
> We own his sentence just.

A broadside that appeared a few days before the hanging of Levi Ames in 1773 mentioned the crowd that would undoubtedly show up for the event. It also identified the different feelings—respectful sympathy and crude enjoyment—that spectators showed at public executions:

See! round the Prison how the Throng
From every Quarter pour;
Some mourn with sympathising Tongue,
The ruder Rabble roar.

And sometimes the lesson was written as if it came
from the condemned criminal himself or herself
(although it probably did not). Levi Ames, for example,
was supposed to have said, after reflecting on his crime
and punishment:

The dreadful Deed for which I die.
Arose from small Beginning;
My idleness brought poverty
And so I took to Stealing.

public executions in New York State. In 1834, New York became the first state to start performing its executions out of public view. This had been another reform urged by Rush: executions, if they must take place, should not be public spectacles but should be carried out in walled enclosures or in yards inside prisons.

Stories about public executions often portray "hanging day" as a kind of mass entertainment during which rowdy, sometimes drunken crowds gathered to watch with voyeuristic satisfaction as a condemned wretch kicked and twitched at the end of the hangman's rope. That image, historians of the death penalty have discovered from studies of old letters, journals, and newspaper accounts, is too simple. Some executions did fit the image of hanging day as a disorderly and rather gruesome festival. But most executions, especially during the seventeenth and eighteenth centuries, were more solemn and somber. They were considered to be religious occasions, with sermons and perhaps even hymns, and the mood was often one of melancholy or awe. Still, officials and ministers fretted that perhaps the large crowds that flocked to executions did not come to ponder the moral lessons that were offered; instead they might be drawn to executions by mere curiosity and the desire to be part of a rare public happening. One observer wrote in 1740, after the hanging of two New Hampshire women for the murder of their children, "Now, tho' *Curiosity* might move many Persons to come and behold those sad Objects, I would charitably hope that many came from a *better Principle*."

Death penalty abolitionists have never agreed on the question of public executions. Some felt in the early nineteenth century—and some still feel—that a deed as serious as the taking of a life by the state should be carried out in public, so that the people can witness the enactment of the public will. Opponents of the death penalty also hoped that public executions would turn people against capital punishment by inspiring feelings of disgust or horror.

The other side of the argument was that public executions stripped the doomed convicts of their last shred of dignity, appealed to low instincts such as curiosity and voyeurism, and were unsuitable community institutions. Like such relics of the barbaric past as gladiatorial combat and bear-baiting, they should be abandoned. This point of view held sway in New York in 1834, when the state banned public executions. Other states followed. By 1849, fifteen of the nation's thirty states had stopped carrying out capital punishment in public.

One of the last public executions in the United States took place in Owensboro, Kentucky, in 1936. Twenty thousand people gathered to watch Rainey Bethea, a twenty-two-year-old African-American man, meet his death by hanging. They tore the hood off his head as a souvenir and cheered as he fell to his death—behavior that surely qualified as an argument against public execution. By that time, however, other methods of execution had been attacked as "cruel and unusual," and the Supreme Court had stepped into the fray.

THree
EXECUTION ON TRIAL

THE WORD "ABOLITIONIST" TODAY calls up the image of someone who opposed slavery, and perhaps worked to end it, before the American Civil War. In the first part of the nineteenth century, though, the term could refer to someone who wanted to see an end to capital punishment. Some activists supported both causes. The Massachusetts Society for the Abolition of Capital Punishment, for example, listed Wendell Phillips and William Lloyd Garrison—major figures in the antislavery movement—among the speakers at its Boston meetings.

The movement against the death penalty gained strength from the 1830s through the early 1850s. It won some significant victories on a state-by-state basis, mostly in the Northern states. These victories took several forms. First, this was the period during which a number of states shifted from public to private executions. Second, some states decapitalized more crimes, which means that they took rape, arson, and other crimes off the lists of offenses that were punishable by death. By 1860, the only capital crimes in any Northern state were treason and murder. The Southern states, in general, kept more capital crimes. Third, some states—starting with Tennessee in 1838—introduced discretionary sentencing. In those states the death penalty was no longer mandatory, or required. Instead, a jury that convicted someone of a capital crime had the power to choose between execution and life in prison as punishment.

The death-penalty abolitionists' goal was to end capital punishment altogether, but they had to settle for partial success. In Maine in 1837, the state legislature passed a law that required a one-year waiting period between a guilty verdict in a capital case and the execution. This gave the strong feelings aroused by a crime and a trial time to cool, and in order for the execution to take place, the governor had to sign a warrant authorizing it. Governors of the state, however, were not eager to

WENDELL PHILLIPS WAS BOTH AN ANTISLAVERY AND ANTI-DEATH PENALTY ACTIVIST IN PRE–CIVIL WAR AMERICA.

go on record as directly responsible for executions. The result was that no executions took place in Maine between 1837 and 1863. Four other Northern states with strong death-penalty abolition movements passed similar "Maine laws."

In 1846 Michigan became the first state to ban capital punishment completely. Rhode Island followed in 1852, Wisconsin in 1853. Around this time, though, the death penalty began to be overshadowed by other issues: the increasingly urgent antislavery movement, the rising tension between Northern and Southern states, and, in 1861, the Civil War.

After the war, the fate of the death penalty followed a somewhat zigzag course as public opinion and lawmakers veered between opposition to capital punishment and support for it. Maine is one example: between 1876 and 1887 it banned capital punishment, then restored it, and finally abolished it again. Iowa did much the same, abolishing the death penalty for six years, then restoring it. Kansas took a different route. In 1872 it passed a "Maine law" that suspended capital punishment without legally abolishing it.

Not until the early twentieth century would more states tackle the issue of capital punishment—still in an on-again, off-again way. Starting in 1907, nine states and Puerto Rico abolished the death penalty. Within a few years, some of those states restored it.

Whether to apply the death penalty, and for what crimes, was decided by the legislative bodies of the individual states. The issue of *how* to apply the death penalty, however, had been raised before the U.S. Supreme Court, whose ruling was binding for the entire nation.

THE SUPREME COURT AND THE DEATH PENALTY

Back when Congress debated whether or not to adopt the Bill of Rights, several representatives worried that the phrase "cruel and unusual punishments" in the Eighth Amendment was so vague that it would cause confusion. It took nearly a century for their fears to be realized, but in 1878 the Supreme Court of the United States heard a case that challenged a death sentence on the grounds that it was cruel and unusual.

When the Supreme Court hears cases that have been appealed to it from lower courts, it is rarely concerned with the question of guilt or innocence. Its concern is with questions of constitutionality—that is, with whether a law or an action has violated the U.S. Constitution. The Supreme Court overturns the verdict of a lower court only if it finds that the lower court arrived at its verdict unconstitutionally. So when the attorneys for a man named Wallace Wilkerson brought his case to the Supreme Court, they did not challenge the decision of the Utah Territory jury that had found Wilkerson guilty of premeditated murder.

Wilkerson v. *Utah* concerned the sentence that the judge had pronounced on Wilkerson: "that between the hours of ten o'clock in the forenoon and three o'clock in the afternoon of [December 14] you be taken from your place of confinement to some place within this district, and that you there be publicly shot until you are dead." It had been unconstitutional for the judge to select Wilkerson's punishment, Wilkerson's lawyers claimed. In addition, being shot to death was a cruel and unusual method of execution.

The Supreme Court of the Utah Territory had already upheld the judge's sentence. Now the U.S. Supreme Court upheld the decision of the territorial supreme court. It ruled that the judge had acted properly, and within the scope of his duties, in delivering Wilkerson's sentence. It also ruled that the judge had no legal duty to sentence Wilkerson to hanging, which was the more usual mode of execution, and that being shot to death was not a cruel and unusual punishment. Shooting had to be considered defensible as a mode of execution because it was accepted by legal authorities for use in certain military crimes, such as disobedience, desertion, and mutiny.

The Supreme Court recognized that it would be difficult to determine just how far the Eighth Amendment's prohibition on cruel and unusual punishments was supposed to reach. Torture and unnecessary cruelty were clearly forbidden, however. Death by shooting did not fall into either of those categories, so it was permissible. Wilkerson's execution by firing squad should proceed.

Wilkerson was the Supreme Court's first brush with the Eighth Amendment. Twelve years later, in 1890, the Court again grappled with the death penalty. This time the punishment under challenge was not the firing squad or some other familiar, traditional form of execution. It was a new and unknown piece of technology: the electric chair.

One reason that some people opposed the death penalty was the pain and suffering inflicted during executions. That concern could even change the law. Wisconsin abolished the death penalty in 1853, for example, after a notorious execution in which the victim struggled for five minutes after he was hanged, and another thirteen minutes passed before his heart stopped. Such incidents were not uncommon. Hanging had always resulted in some prolonged or especially painful deaths. By the late nineteenth century, however, people were less willing to tolerate the inconsistency and occasional slow suffocation of hanging. Experiments with new methods of hanging people that used longer, more forceful drops didn't solve the problem; in fact, they produced a stream of horrific executions in which criminals' heads were violently ripped from their bodies.

In 1880 the *New York Times* suggested that the United States should adopt the guillotine as a better, more consistent method of execution than hanging. That suggestion was never adopted, but eight years later, a new method of killing criminals appeared. It employed electricity, the newly mastered force that was transforming American life and industry.

THE ELECTRIC CHAIR

Electrocution (a combination of *electricity* and *execution*) was one result of a bitter commercial feud between Thomas Alva Edison and George Westinghouse. Each was an inventor and businessman who wanted to sell electrical equipment and systems to cities, and each championed a different system. Edison's equipment used a form of electrical transmission called direct current, or DC; Westinghouse's used alternating current, or AC.

AC's chief disadvantage was that it was deadlier than DC to someone accidentally exposed to the current. During the 1880s, Edison and his company exploited this fact in demonstrations designed to promote DC. They highlighted the dangers of AC by killing animals with it. At the same time, people in England were adopting electricity as a method of slaughtering livestock; it was thought to be more merciful than the axe. Meanwhile, prison guards in Ohio had taken to disciplining unruly prisoners with electrical shocks. It was a short step to the idea of using electricity to kill condemned prisoners.

New York was the first state to investigate the possibilities of execution by electricity. In 1886 the legislature appointed a committee to research "the most humane and practical method known to modern science of carrying into effect the sentence of death." In January 1888 the committee turned in its report. After considering thirty-four ways of killing, it recommended electricity, which could be administered quite economically through "a chair, with a head and foot-rest." With help from Edison's laboratory, an engineer named Harold P. Brown built the first electric chair. It used AC. (An associate of Edison proposed that executing prisoners with AC could be called "westinghousing" them, but the term never caught on.)

The electric chair seemed to represent science, progress, and a method of execution that was both tidy and humane. By 1889 it was ready for its first use. The condemned criminal scheduled to make death-penalty history was William Kemmler of Buffalo, New York, who had been convicted of murdering his girlfriend. But two weeks before Kemmler was supposed to die in the chair, attorneys acting on his behalf filed a motion to prevent the execution. Death by electricity, they claimed, was cruel and unusual punishment, which was prohibited by New York's state constitution. This launched a yearlong legal process that would reach the U.S. Supreme Court. It also marked the beginning of a mystery that is not fully solved to this day.

Electrocution was certainly unusual. In fact, it was completely novel. But was it cruel? The chief witnesses who testified on that question before the court were Thomas A. Edison, who had fervently supported the use of the AC electric chair, and Harold P. Brown, who had built the chair and conducted many electrocution tests on animals. After hearing a lot of testimony, the court found no reason to think that death by electric chair would be more painful than hanging, so it upheld Kemmler's sentence. His attorneys took the case to a New York State appeals court, which upheld the sentence. Then they took it to the state supreme court. It upheld the sentence, too.

Kemmler's attorneys carried the matter all the way to the U.S. Supreme Court. They argued that the State of New York had violated Kemmler's constitutional rights under the Fourteenth Amendment, which had become law in 1868. The Fourteenth Amendment prevents the states from depriving citizens of life, liberty, or property without due process of law. The attorneys claimed that the legislature of New York had broken the Fourteenth Amendment when it made the cruel and unusual punishment of electrocution the state's method of judicial execution, a method not used in any other state.

The Court found that the New York legislature had not acted unconstitutionally, and that the state supreme court had been right to uphold Kemmler's sentence. In its May 1890 ruling, the U.S. Supreme Court noted:

> Punishments are cruel when they involve torture or a lingering death; but the punishment of death

is not cruel within the meaning of that word as used in the constitution. It implies there something inhuman and barbarous,—something more than the mere extinguishment of life. . . . In order to reverse the judgment of the highest court of the state of New York, we should be compelled to hold that it had committed an error so gross as to amount in law to a denial by the state of due process of law to one accused of crime, or of some right secured to him by the constitution of the United States. We have no hesitation in saying that this we cannot do upon the record before us.

The Supreme Court may have ruled that electrocution was constitutionally permissible, but that did not guarantee that the first electrocution would go smoothly. Kemmler's execution on August 6, 1890, was attended by twenty-five witnesses, including a representative of a newspaper association and several doctors. No doubt all of them were aware that they were present at an historic occasion. Kemmler cordially wished them all good luck, and then the current flowed through the chair and into Kemmler's body for seventeen seconds.

Afterward, the witnesses saw with horror that Kemmler was still breathing. A second charge of current was hurriedly administered. This time the technicians, fearful of making another mistake, kept the current on for so long that Kemmler's hair started to singe. The odor of burned flesh filled the room. The New York Times delivered its verdict the next day with a shocking headline: "Far Worse Than Hanging: Kemmler's Death Proves an Awful Spectacle."

The newspapers also speculated about a mystery behind Kemmler's series of appeals. Kemmler was represented by several well-known, expensive lawyers, but he was poor. So who was paying his attorneys? (The states had not yet begun the practice of providing court-appointed public defenders for people who could not afford lawyers.) The newspapers and the public jumped to the conclusion that George Westinghouse was funding Kemmler's appeals because he wanted to prevent his AC electrical system from being tainted by association with the death penalty. Westinghouse denied it. His company's in-house attorney suggested, rather unconvincingly, that some unknown person had "started this proceeding because it involves an interesting

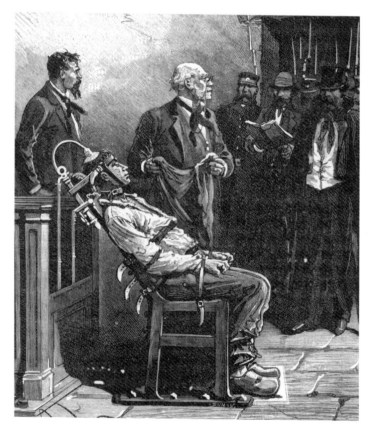

THE FIRST PERSON EXECUTED IN THE ELECTRIC CHAIR WAS CONVICTED MURDERER WILLIAM KEMMLER, ON AUGUST 6, 1890.

point of law, and simply for the fun of it." No definite evidence has ever emerged to link Westinghouse with the Kemmler case, or to show who paid Kemmler's attorneys to conduct the appeal process.

If Westinghouse was behind the appeals, he must have viewed the Supreme Court's ruling as a setback. The Court not did not ban the use of the electric chair. Yet in spite of all Edison's efforts to link AC with the death penalty (and with the danger of accidental electrocution), AC eventually became the basis of the nation's electrical systems because it is cheaper to produce than DC.

And in spite of the unfortunate events at the electrocution of William Kemmler, the electric chair was established as a new method of administering capital punishment. New York electrocuted another twenty people by the end of 1893. Three years after that, Ohio adopted the electric chair. Other states followed throughout the first half of the twentieth century. Some electrical engineers and physicians argued that electrocution was not always fatal and that some of the convicts who were subjected to it actually died afterward, during their autopsies. These concerns, never clearly proven, did not halt the spread of the electric chair.

Electrocutions could be disturbing, even appalling, but overall most people considered them more humane than hanging. But like hanging, electrocution would gradually give way to new, more humane methods of execution. In 1923, Nevada became the first state to carry out an execution by lethal gas. It used cyanide gas to kill a condemned murderer inside a sealed chamber. Lethal injection, in which toxic drugs are injected into the condemned person's veins to bring unconsciousness and then death, was pioneered in Oklahoma in 1977. Lethal injection has become the most commonly used method of execution in the United States.

ANOTHER POPULAR METHOD OF EXECUTION IN THE TWENTIETH CENTURY WAS
THE GAS CHAMBER. PICTURED HERE IS THE INTERIOR OF THE GAS CHAMBER
USED IN CALIFORNIA'S SAN QUENTIN PRISON.

"HUMANE JUSTICE" AND THE "DIGNITY OF MAN"

While the nation's execution chambers adapted to new
technologies during the first part of the twentieth century, the justices of the U.S. Supreme Court delivered a
series of rulings that had important effects on capital
punishment in America. One of the most significant cases
was *Weems* v. *United States* (1910), which didn't even
involve the death penalty.

Paul A. Weems was a Coast Guard officer in the Philippines who was sentenced to fifteen years of "hard and painful labor" in prison, as well as lifetime surveillance after leaving prison, for falsifying a public document (records of cash payments to lighthouse employees). His case was appealed to the U.S. Supreme Court on the grounds that the penalties violated the Eighth Amendment. The most significant aspect of the Court's ruling lay in two different interpretations of the amendment's ban on "cruel and unusual punishments."

Two of the justices, Oliver Wendell Holmes Jr. and Edward D. White, interpreted the ban to refer only to punishments that were cruel and unusual when the amendment was adopted into law in 1791. On this basis, they ruled that Weems's sentence did not violate the Eighth Amendment. Hard and painful labor followed by surveillance, they declared, would not have been considered cruel and unusual in the late eighteenth century.

The other seven justices, however, took a broader view of "cruel and unusual." They interpreted it to mean punishments that were cruel and unusual by the standards of society when the crime was committed and the case was heard. In other words, they saw the Eighth Amendment as keeping pace with the times. As society's standards changed, so did the interpretation of the amendment. The Court could not be expected to enforce the eighteenth century's version of punishment forever.

Justice Joseph McKenna summed up the majority opinion:

> Legislation, both statutory and constitutional, is enacted, it is true, from an experience of evils but its general language should not, therefore, be necessarily confined to the form that evil had theretofore taken. Time works changes, brings into

existence new conditions and purposes. Therefore a principle, to be vital, must be capable of wider application than the mischief which gave it birth. This is peculiarly true of constitutions. They are not ephemeral enactments, designed to meet passing occasions. They are, to use the words of Chief Justice Marshall, "designed to approach immortality as nearly as human institutions can approach it." The future is their care, and provision for events of good and bad tendencies of which no prophecy can be made. In the application of a constitution, therefore, our contemplation cannot be only of what has been, but of what may be.

The Court overturned Weems's sentence by a majority of 7 to 2. In McKenna's words, it had ruled that the interpretation of the Eighth Amendment "may acquire meaning as public opinion becomes enlightened by a humane justice." *Weems* had established the principle that the definition of "cruel and unusual" was not fixed in time but could change to reflect society's more "humane" views.

A failure of the electric chair led to the strange case of *Francis* v. *Resweber*, decided by the U.S. Supreme Court in 1947. Willie Francis was convicted of murder in Louisiana and sentenced to death. At the time, Louisiana executed its criminals in the electric chair. Francis went to his execution on the appointed date. The switch was thrown, but the current did not kill him—the equipment had malfunctioned. Francis was led back to his cell to await a new execution date, six days later.

An attorney for Francis filed an appeal in state court, and Francis received a stay of execution so that the appeal could be heard. As the petitioner, the party who requested the supreme court to hear the case, Francis based his appeal on constitutional grounds. One ground was the

THE COURT OF PUBLIC OPINION

Two media events in the middle of the twentieth century turned many Americans against the death penalty. One was a book, the other a movie. Each portrayed a condemned convict in a somewhat sympathetic light.

The book was *Cell 2455, Death Row*, published in 1954. It was written in prison by a man named Caryl Chessman while he was awaiting the death penalty in California for kidnapping. Chessman used the proceeds from the sale of the book to hire lawyers to appeal his case. While the appeals went on for another six years, Chessman wrote several more books and became a center of international attention. Many people believed he was innocent of the crimes for which he had been convicted (he had confessed to them, but later said that the police had tortured him to get the confession). Others thought he was probably guilty but deserved life in prison rather than execution because he hadn't committed murder. People from all over the world and all walks of life—from the queen of Belgium to evangelist Billy Graham—pleaded for a commutation of Chessman's sentence. But Chessman's appeals, and his time, ran out in 1960, and he was executed in the gas chamber at San Quentin Prison.

The movie was called *I Want to Live!* It was released in 1958, at the height of the anti-death penalty feeling stirred up by the Chessman case. Directed by Robert Wise, the film was based on the death of Barbara Graham, who had been executed at San Quentin three years earlier. Graham, an occasional prostitute, had been convicted of murder after she and four male accomplices robbed an elderly, crippled woman; Graham beat the woman to

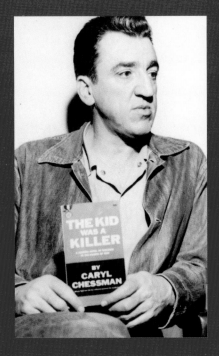

death with a gun butt during the robbery. Like Chessman, Graham had been the subject of pleas and protests from death-penalty opponents—in her case this was partly because some people objected to executing women. *I Want to Live!* starred the very popular actress Susan Hayward as Graham in a role that downplayed Graham's sordid past and the brutal details of her crime, emphasizing her psychological suffering on Death Row.

During the 1950s, public opinion in America started shifting away from support for capital punishment. *Cell 2455, Death Row* and *I Want to Live!* were part of that shift. A decade later, William Henry Furman, whose statement about his own Death Row appeal—"I just wanted to stay alive"—seems to echo the desperate cry of Hayward's character in the film, would be the key to ending the death penalty . . . for a while.

Fifth Amendment, which prohibits double jeopardy—in other words, it says that no one can be tried or punished twice for the same crime. Another was the Eighth Amendment. Francis claimed that the ordeal of preparing for a second time to be executed would be cruel and unusual punishment. Finally, the petitioner argued that being deprived of his rights under the Fifth and Eighth Amendments would amount to a violation of his right to due process of law under the Fourteenth Amendment.

Louisiana's supreme court denied the appeal. Francis's attorney then took *Francis* v. *Resweber* to the U.S. Supreme Court. (Resweber's name became attached to the defendant's, or respondent's, side of the case because he was the sheriff who had presided over the attempted execution.) Justice Stanley F. Reed wrote the Court's opinion. He began by recognizing the highly unusual nature of the case, saying, "So far as we are aware, this case is without precedent in any court."

The Court found that neither the Fifth Amendment nor the Eighth Amendment had been violated in Francis's case, which meant that the Fourteenth Amendment did not apply either. Even though Francis might suffer additional pain as a result of a delayed execution, the pain was caused by an accident, not inflicted by the state as part of the punishment. Wrote Reed:

> Petitioner's suggestion is that because he once underwent the psychological strain of preparation for electrocution, now to require him to undergo this preparation again subjects him to a lingering or cruel and unusual punishment. Even the fact that petitioner has already been subjected to a current of electricity does not make his subsequent execution any more cruel in the constitutional sense than any other execution. The cruelty

against which the Constitution protects a convicted man is cruelty inherent in the method of
punishment, not the necessary suffering involved
in any method employed to extinguish life
humanely. The fact that an unforeseeable accident
prevented the prompt consummation of the sentence cannot, it seems to us, add an element of
cruelty to a subsequent execution. There is no purpose to inflict unnecessary pain nor any unnecessary pain involved in the proposed execution. The
situation of the unfortunate victim of this accident
is just as though he had suffered the identical
amount of mental anguish and physical pain in any
other occurrence, such as, for example, a fire in
the cell block. We cannot agree that the hardship
imposed upon the petitioner rises to that level of
hardship denounced as denial of due process
because of cruelty.

The Supreme Court had ruled in *Weems* that the interpretation of the Eighth Amendment should change to
reflect "new conditions" in society. That concept was
strengthened by another Supreme Court decision in 1958.
The case of *Trop* v. *Dulles* concerned Albert Trop, who had
been convicted of desertion during World War II. As punishment, he had been denationalized, or stripped of his
U.S. citizenship. John Foster Dulles was named as the
respondent in the case because he was the U.S. secretary of
state at the time.

The Court determined that Trop's punishment was
excessive and that the national government did not pos-
sess the power to take away citizenship. Wrote Chief
Justice Earl Warren, "Citizenship is not a license that
expires upon misbehavior."

Warren also wrote:

The basic concept underlying the Eighth Amendment is nothing less than the dignity of man. While the State has the power to punish, the Amendment stands to assure that this power be exercised within the limits of civilized standards. Fines, imprisonment and even execution may be imposed depending upon the enormity of the crime, but any technique outside the bounds of these traditional penalties is constitutionally suspect. This Court has had little occasion to give precise content to the Eighth Amendment, and, in an enlightened democracy such as ours, this is not surprising.

Then, referring to *Weems* v. *United States*, Warren pointed out that in 1910 the Supreme Court had not hesitated to identify a penalty as cruel and unusual. "The Court recognized in that case that the words of the Amendment are not precise, and that their scope is not static," he declared. "The Amendment must draw its meaning from the evolving standards of decency that mark the progress of a maturing society."

Although *Trop* had not involved execution, opponents of the death penalty seized on Chief Justice Warren's use of the phrase "evolving standards." Warren had repeated the principle that interpretations of the Eighth Amendment could change over time as society's attitudes changed. Even though the death penalty had been found constitutional in the past, the Court was not bound by those earlier decisions. Punishments that had once been considered ordinary, such as burning, branding, and cutting off ears, were no longer used—in fact, they were viewed as barbaric and cruel. If a case could be made that society had come to regard execution itself as barbaric and cruel, the death penalty might be abolished.

four
CONSTITUTIONAL CHALLENGES TO CAPITAL PUNISHMENT

CAPITAL PUNISHMENT in the United States had always been a state-by-state patchwork. Some states had done away with the death penalty in the nineteenth or early twentieth centuries. A number of them had later reinstated it. Then, during the 1950s and 1960s, a handful of states abolished capital punishment (in the same period, the death penalty was also abolished in many nations that were U.S. allies, including Canada, Great Britain, New Zealand, Australia, and most western European countries).

The majority of American states still had the death penalty by the middle of the twentieth century, but their statutory codes—the lists of crimes that could carry the death penalty—varied wildly. In some states only murder was punishable by death. In others, crimes such as rape, armed robbery, and perjury in a capital case were subject to capital punishment. All in all, more than three dozen crimes carried the death penalty in one state or another.

Executions, however, were on the decline. They had reached their highest rate during the 1930s, with an average of 167 each year. This fell to an average of 129 a year during the 1940s. In the 1950s the average number of executions fell still further, to only 71.5 a year. Yet the number of new death sentences being issued did not fall nearly as sharply. Between 1935 and 1942, an average of

142 convicted criminals each year had been sentenced to die. During the 1960s, the average annual number of new death sentences was 113. More people were being sentenced to death than were being executed.

Some of the condemned criminals received clemency, or mercy, from the governors of their states. Their death sentences were commuted to prison terms. Nationwide information about clemency and commutation is not available for the period before 1960, when the Justice Department started collecting data, but during the 1960s about 15 percent of the people who were sentenced to capital punishment saw their sentences commuted. Legal historian Stuart Banner believes that the rate of clemency in earlier eras was probably higher.

Another key reason for the gap between the number of death sentences and the number of executions was that a multitude of new laws and judicial procedures in the 1950s and 1960s made it easier for condemned criminals to appeal their convictions. With requests for stays of execution, motions for retrials, and formal appeals to higher courts, a prisoner could keep the appeals process going for years, and many of those who persisted in the appeals process had their sentences overturned. Banner credits the increased rate of appeals, rather than a profound change in public opinion, for most of the great decrease in the number of executions by the late 1960s.

Yet judges and juries had become somewhat more reluctant to impose the death penalty, and their reluctance seemed to reflect the opinion of a growing segment of the American people. In 1966 a Gallup poll showed that only 42 percent of the population supported capital punishment, while 47 percent opposed it. This was the first time that such a poll had found more Americans against the death penalty than for it. It would also be the last time—but death-penalty abolitionists had no way of knowing that. They believed that the end of the death penalty was within reach.

Just two executions took place in the United States in 1967, the year William Henry Furman committed murder in Savannah, Georgia. Furman's case happened at a time when the American public seemed readier than it had ever been to eliminate the death penalty. The *Furman* case also coincided with a new phase of the legal assault on capital punishment.

A NEW APPROACH TO ABOLITION

In the 1960s, the movement to abolish the death penalty in the United States went through "a major transformation," in the words of legal scholar and death-penalty abolitionist Hugo Adam Bedau. Before that time, the question of whether a particular offense was subject to capital punishment, or whether capital punishment was permissible at all, had been decided by lawmakers. State legislatures determined the states' statutory codes, and the U.S. Congress did so for federal crimes. The death-penalty abolitionists' new strategy was to shift the battle from the legislatures to the courtrooms—specifically to the U.S. Supreme Court, where it would be fought on constitutional grounds.

The Supreme Court had reviewed constitutional issues connected with the death penalty before. The *Wilkerson, Kemmler,* and *Francis* cases, though, had been concerned with the details of particular punishments. The attorneys who had brought those cases to the Court had hoped for nothing more far-reaching than saving their clients from execution. In the 1960s—an era of sweeping social changes, protests, and challenges to established norms such as racism—the goal was more ambitious. Opponents of capital punishment wanted the Supreme Court to strike down the death penalty itself.

In late 1967 the Court agreed to hear the case of *United*

States v. *Jackson*. Stephen Duke, a law professor at Yale University, represented Charles Jackson and two other men who had been convicted of kidnapping. Their crime fell under the Federal Kidnapping Act, which decreed that anyone found guilty under the Act "shall be punished (1) by death if the kidnaped [sic] person has not been liberated unharmed, and if the verdict of the jury shall so recommend, or (2) by imprisonment for any term of years or for life, if the death penalty is not imposed."

Duke had spotted a loophole in the language of the Kidnapping Act. The law allowed the death penalty *if* the jury recommended it, but the law said nothing about the death penalty in cases where there was *no* jury (if the defendant pled guilty, or waived the right to a jury trial and agreed to be tried and sentenced by a judge). Duke argued that this meant that defendants who insisted upon their constitutional right to a jury trial, which is guaranteed under the Sixth Amendment, risked the death penalty, while defendants who gave up that right escaped the death penalty. The effect was to discourage defendants from demanding jury trials—and thus, perhaps, preventing them from convincing a jury of their innocence. This, Duke claimed, violated the Fourteenth Amendment's protection of due process, or equal treatment under the law, for all.

The Supreme Court agreed with Duke. It found the capital-punishment clause of the Federal Kidnapping Act unconstitutional and invalid. The Court's finding in *United States* v. *Jackson* had a domino effect on other legislation. The same faulty, unconstitutional language was found in the death-penalty clauses of several other federal laws, as well as the death-sentencing laws of ten states. All were invalidated and rewritten.

THE DEATH-QUALIFIED JURY

Another Supreme Court ruling in 1968 was important for the future of the death penalty. It focused on the way juries were selected in capital trials. *Witherspoon* v. *Illinois* concerned the case of William C. Witherspoon, who had been convicted of murder and sentenced to death in Illinois. Witherspoon's attorney, Albert Jenner of Chicago, appealed both the conviction and the sentence on the ground that the jury, which had delivered both the guilty verdict and the death sentence, had been unconstitutionally selected.

Illinois law allowed the prosecutors in capital cases to eliminate anyone from the jury pool who was opposed to the death penalty, or even had doubts about it. In Witherspoon's case, nearly half of the prospective jurors had been eliminated from the pool of possibilities after prosecutors questioned them about their views on the death penalty.

WILLIAM C. WITHERSPOON WAS CONVICTED OF, AND SENTENCED TO DEATH FOR, MURDER, BUT BEFORE HE DIED, HIS CASE WENT TO THE SUPREME COURT. THAT CASE BECAME A MILESTONE WHEN THE SUPREME COURT RULED THAT ANY PROSPECTIVE JUROR WHO DECLARED THAT HE OR SHE WAS COMPLETELY OPPOSED TO THE DEATH PENALTY COULD BE STRUCK FROM THE JURY.

Jenner argued that the jury-selection law resulted in juries made up *only* of people who supported the death penalty. This affected more than the sentencing of convicted criminals. It also affected whether or not they were found guilty in the first place, Jenner claimed. He tried to show that jurors who favored the death penalty were more likely to find defendants guilty than people who were neutral about the death penalty, had doubts about it, or were opposed to it. This meant that the jury that had tried and sentenced Witherspoon was slanted toward the death penalty. It was a hanging jury.

The jury-selection process challenged in *Witherspoon* v. *Illinois* was not unique to Illinois, nor was it new. It had been used for many years in every jurisdiction that had capital crimes. The idea behind it was to make sure that the jury in a capital case did not include someone so strongly opposed to the death penalty that he or she would refuse to convict a defendant if the conviction would result in execution—no matter what facts emerged during the course of the trial, and even if the juror thought that the defendant was guilty. In other words, jury selection winnowed out death-penalty opponents because they might refuse, or be unable, to carry out their duty of pronouncing a guilty verdict and/or applying a death sentence.

But in eliminating all prospective jurors with doubts about the death penalty, Jenner claimed on behalf of Witherspoon, the state had gone too far. The Sixth and Fourteenth Amendments to the Constitution guaranteed a fair trial, but Witherspoon had been deprived of a fair trial by a jury-selection process that slanted the outcome toward conviction and execution. Jenner asked the U.S. Supreme Court to reverse not just his client's death sentence but his guilty verdict as well. And Witherspoon's verdict was not the only one at stake. If the Court overturned that verdict, then hundreds, possibly thousands, of guilty verdicts that had been delivered by similar juries must also be overturned.

The justices of the Supreme Court decided not to rule on the constitutionality of Witherspoon's guilty verdict. Although research in the social sciences did appear to support Jenner's claim that jurors who supported the death penalty were more likely than other jurors to find defendants guilty, that research was preliminary, and there was not much of it. The Court did not have enough information to rule on the question of conviction by a pro-death penalty jury. Justice Potter Stewart, who wrote the Court's opinion, explained:

> We simply cannot conclude, either on the basis of the record now before us or as a matter of judicial notice, that the exclusion of jurors opposed to capital punishment results in an unrepresentative jury on the issue of guilt or substantially increases the risk of conviction. In light of the presently available information, we are not prepared to announce a per se constitutional rule requiring the reversal of every conviction returned by a jury selected as this one was.

With the question of conviction out of the way, the Court turned its attention to the matter of Witherspoon's death sentence. There it did deliver a ruling. It examined the Illinois law that allowed prosecutors to challenge, or reject, jurors. The law said: "In trials for murder it shall be a cause for challenge of any juror who shall, on being examined, state that he has conscientious scruples against capital punishment, or that he is opposed to the same." This law, the Court ruled, was too broad.

In the opinion of the Court, a state could eliminate prospective jurors who declared that they were absolutely opposed to the death penalty and would never consider returning a verdict that would result in death. The state could not, however, eliminate people simply because they had doubts or "scruples" about the death penalty. The state had no way of knowing that someone with moral or religious qualms about capital punishment, even someone who was opposed to the death penalty in principle, would not perform his or her duty on a given jury. An opponent of the death penalty should be considered as capable of performing that duty as a supporter of it, unless the opponent said in no uncertain words that he or she would never apply the death penalty. In a nation "less than half of whose people believe in the death penalty," as Stewart put it, juries should not be made up only of believers. This would mean that they were not representative of the community and society as a whole.

"In its quest for a jury capable of imposing the death penalty, the State produced a jury uncommonly willing to condemn a man to die," wrote Stewart in the *Witherspoon* opinion. He concluded, "Whatever else might be said of capital punishment, it is at least clear that its imposition by a hanging jury cannot be squared with the Constitution. The State of Illinois has stacked the deck against the petitioner. To execute this death sentence would deprive him of his life without due process of law."

When the Court overturned Witherspoon's death sentence, it *vacated*, or invalidated, many other sentences as well. Most of those condemned criminals received new sentencing hearings, under jury-selection procedures that had been written to meet the standard set in *Witherspoon* v. *Illinois*. That standard remains in force today. A jury that meets the standard may or may not include people who are opposed to capital punishment in principle, but it may not include anyone who is completely against the death penalty under any and all circumstances.

Such a jury is said to be *death qualified* (or, occasionally, *witherspooned*).

Both *Jackson* and *Witherspoon* could be seen as blows against capital punishment. Both cases, however, turned on matters of procedure. They were concerned with how the death penalty was applied, not with whether it could be applied at all. Despite the high hopes of attorneys and activists working to abolish capital punishment, the Supreme Court had yet to hear a case that challenged the death penalty itself.

About three and a half months after the Supreme Court issued its ruling against "hanging juries" in *Witherspoon* v. *Illinois*, William Henry Furman's murder trial took place in Georgia, and Furman received the death sentence. His attorney, B. Clarence Mayfield, tried to use *Witherspoon* to his client's advantage in his appeal. He argued that Furman's jury was improperly slanted toward the death penalty, but his argument failed to convince the Georgia Supreme Court, which upheld Furman's verdict and death sentence.

Defeated in the state courts, Mayfield prepared to take *Furman* v. *Georgia* to the next level of appeal. Although Mayfield had been Furman's lawyer from the start, he would be just one of seven attorneys to petition the U.S. Supreme Court to hear *Furman*. The other six were members of the Legal Defense and Educational Fund (LDF), an organization that had been deeply involved in bringing the issue of capital punishment before the nation's highest court. The LDF's interest in capital punishment grew out of another powerful reform movement of the mid-twentieth century: the civil rights movement.

THE CIVIL RIGHTS CONNECTION
The National Association for the Advancement of Colored People (NAACP) had fought racial discrimination ever

THURGOOD MARSHALL STARTED AS A CIVIL-RIGHTS ATTORNEY AND ENDED UP
ON THE SUPREME COURT.

since it was founded in 1909. The members of the NAACP,
both black and white, were leaders in the movement to end
racial segregation and to bring about other civil-rights
reforms. The NAACP's legal arm was the LDF, which pur-
sued social and racial justice in the courts.

Guided by an attorney named Thurgood Marshall, the LDF
won one of its biggest victories in 1954, when the Supreme
Court ruled, in *Brown* v. *Board of Education*, to outlaw seg-
regation in the nation's public schools. President
Lyndon B. Johnson made Marshall the first African-
American justice of the Supreme Court in 1967. In the

years that followed, under the leadership of attorney Jack Greenberg, the LDF supported or participated in hundreds of death-penalty appeals.

The LDF had first approached the death penalty as a civil-rights issue, arguing that black defendants in criminal cases were treated differently than white ones, especially in the southern states. It had focused on rape cases, because the element of racial inequity was obvious in such cases: a high percentage of those executed for rape were black men who had been convicted of raping white women.

The LDF had appealed the verdicts of a 1949 case in which seven black men received the death sentence for raping a white woman in Martinsville, Virginia. It tried to show that the death sentences were unconstitutional because they violated the Fourteenth Amendment's guarantee of equal protection for all under the law. The application of the death penalty, the LDF argued, was discriminatory. This argument failed, however, because the LDF could not prove that the jurors had demonstrated intentional racial discrimination.

The Martinsville case had not reached the Supreme Court, but in the late 1960s the LDF succeeded in getting the Court to hear some of its death-penalty cases. A key figure in making that happen was Supreme Court Justice Arthur Goldberg, an experienced labor attorney whom President Kennedy appointed to the Supreme Court in 1962.

During his first year on the Court, Goldberg was troubled by the flood of appeals that asked the justices to review death-penalty cases. Eleven years later he would write in the *Arizona Law Review*, "I found disturbing evidence that the imposition of the death penalty was arbitrary, haphazard, capricious, and discriminatory. The impact of the death penalty was demonstrably greatest among disadvantaged minorities." Goldberg wanted to be ready to write a well-informed opinion on the constitutional aspects of capital punishment when a suitable case came before the Court. He assigned his law clerk to research the subject and write a paper on it. The clerk's name was Alan Dershowitz; he would later become well known as a defense attorney in criminal cases.

"I turned to the books with a sense of mission," Dershowitz said of the assignment Goldberg had given him. "Here was a real opportunity for the Supreme Court to save countless lives." The result was a thorough review of ways that the death penalty might be found unconstitutional. Goldberg used much of Dershowitz's work in a memorandum, or paper, that he sent to the other eight justices of the Court in October 1963.

"I propose to raise the following issue," the memorandum began. "Whether, and under what circumstances, the imposition of the death penalty is proscribed [banned] by the Eighth and Fourteenth Amendments to the United States Constitution." Goldberg was looking for an opportunity to challenge the death penalty. He raised the *Weems* and *Trop* cases, which had established the idea that interpretations of "cruel and unusual punishment" should change to match "evolving standards of decency."

Had standards of decency evolved past the death penalty? Goldberg argued that they had, and that modern attitudes saw "the deliberate institutionalized taking of human life by the state" as "barbaric and inhuman." He pointed to the fact that "many, if not most, of the civilized nations of the western world" had abolished the death penalty. (This argument has traditionally had little effect on American supporters of capital punishment, who reject the notion that the United States should be guided in its domestic affairs by the standards of other countries.) Goldberg then argued that the Court did not have to wait until the American public overwhelmingly condemned capital punishment. It could lead the way. He wrote, "In certain matters—especially those relating to fair procedures in criminal trials—this Court traditionally has guided rather than followed public opinion in the process of articulating and establishing progressively civilized standards of decency."

The memorandum alerted the Court to the fact that its newest member was on a mission. The reactions of the other justices varied. Chief Justice Earl Warren was angry. He felt that Goldberg's clear interest in challenging the death penalty, if it became public, would turn people against the Court. The Supreme Court was already unpopular with many people for its controversial decision in *Brown* v. *Board of Education* and its continued efforts to enforce school desegregation. It had its hands full with that issue, Warren thought, and should not risk alienating the public still further at the moment. John Harlan agreed that it was a bad time to raise the issue of the death penalty. Hugo Black went further. He was, he declared, firmly against Goldberg's ideas.

Two justices, William J. Brennan and William O. Douglas, had a different response. They shared Goldberg's concerns about capital punishment and felt that he had raised some good points. Soon after Goldberg issued the memorandum, *Rudolph* v. *Alabama* gave the three justices an opportunity to express their views. The case involved a black man who had received the death sentence for rape. It was one of many cases presented to the Court in 1963.

The Supreme Court can agree to hear only a fraction of the cases submitted to it. In 1960, for example, more than 2,300 cases were appealed or otherwise presented to the Court. Usually, a case appears in the form of a request from the petitioner for a writ of *certiorari*. This Latin legal term refers to an order that authorizes the moving of records

CHIEF JUSTICE EARL WARREN (*LEFT*) TAKES A WALK WITH NEWLY APPOINTED ASSOCIATE JUSTICE ARTHUR GOLDBERG ON A CRISP FALL DAY IN 1962. ON THE COURT, THE TWO WERE NOT ALWAYS SO CORDIAL.

from a lower court to a higher one. The Supreme Court justices review the requests and decide whether or not to grant *certiorari* in each case.

Their decision takes into account whether the case presents significant or pressing constitutional issues that should be resolved for the public good. The Court might also agree to hear a case if the lower courts have delivered conflicting opinions on it. Before *certiorari* can be granted to a case, four or more justices of the Court must agree to hear it. If a case is not accepted by the minimum of four justices, the Court answers the petitioner's request with a denial of *certiorari*.

Rudolph v. *Alabama* failed to make it onto the Supreme Court's calendar, or list, of accepted cases. Only three justices—Goldberg, Brennan, and Douglas—wanted to hear *Rudolph*. When the Court issued its refusal to hear the case, the document included a dissent, or statement of disagreement with the majority decision. Brennan and Douglas signed the dissent, which Goldberg wrote. It was a very brief version of one of the arguments he had presented in his memorandum, pointing out that the use of the death penalty for a crime such as rape, in which no one had been killed, raised questions connected with the Eighth Amendment's ban on excessive punishments.

The *Rudolph* dissent sent a clear message to the lawyers of the LDF and another civil rights organization, the American Civil Liberties Union (ACLU), which had also been looking for ways to attack the death penalty. Three Supreme Court justices had raised the question of the constitutionality of capital punishment—even though the lawyer for Rudolph, the petitioner, had not asked them to! While the ACLU focused on efforts to get the death penalty abolished by state legislatures, the LDF attorneys were inspired to step up their efforts to bring before the Court a constitutional challenge to the death penalty. In a 1975 biography of her husband, Arthur Goldberg's wife wrote that this was exactly what he had hoped would happen. Goldberg, however, was not part of the Supreme Court when the death-penalty cases started coming. In 1965, at the request of President Lyndon B. Johnson, Goldberg resigned from the Court to serve as the U.S. ambassador to the United Nations.

brings a case to the courts. Also called a plaintiff. See **Petitioner**.

Decapitalization: Removing a crime from the category of offenses punishable by death.

Commutation: The process of changing, or commuting, the sentence of a convicted criminal, such as from death to life imprisonment.

Constitutionality: The question of whether an action is permitted under the U.S. Constitution or is in violation of it. Questions of constitutionality are decided by the U.S. Supreme Court.

Death qualification: Questioning potential jurors to determine whether they are completely unwilling to impose the death penalty, and rejecting them if they are.

Defendant or **defense**: The one against whom a complaint is made; the side that defends against a lawsuit. See **Respondent**.

Discrimination: Act of singling out a group or groups of people for worse treatment than others receive, or judging them by different standards.

Dissent: Disagreement or departure from the majority opinion. Justices who disagree with a majority ruling of the Court may write dissenting opinions that explain their positions.

Due process: A right guaranteed to all citizens under the Fifth and Fourteenth Amendments of the Constitution, which state that the law will be applied to all citizens in the same way, in all circumstances.

Equal protection: A right guaranteed to all citizens under the Fourteenth Amendment of the Constitution, which says that all citizens must receive the same protection of the laws, regardless of race, color, creed, or the fact that they were formerly slaves.

Felony murder: Killing someone during, or as a result of, another crime, such as burglary.

Majority: In Supreme Court cases, five out of nine justices. See **Swing vote**.

Malice aforethought: The intention to do harm (malice is ill-will); killing someone with malice aforethought is held to be a more serious crime than killing someone by accident.

Moot: Without practical significance. A court may decide that a case is moot if a decision will be meaningless or have no effect; in law school, students practice by arguing cases in mock or moot court.

Petitioner: Party who brings a case before the U.S. Supreme Court. See **Complainant**.

Plaintiff: See **Complainant**.

Precedent: Principle established in a previous law case or cases; new cases are often decided on the basis of the precedent set by earlier ones.

Respondent: Second party in a Supreme Court case. See **Defendant**.

Statutory: Having to do with the law.

Stay: A stay of execution is a suspension that occurs when a scheduled execution is put on hold, usually for a specified period so that a legal challenge can be met.

Swing vote: The tiebreaker, or vote that settles a tie between four Supreme Court justices on one side and four on the other.

Unanimous: Agreed to by all. In Supreme Court cases, a unanimous decision, with all nine justices in agreement, is considered more emphatic than a split decision, but it has no more legal force than a simple majority.

Vacate: To invalidate or throw out a convicted person's sentence, usually for legal technicalities.

The five who shared this opinion were Douglas, Warren, Marshall, Abe Fortas, and Brennan. While they were waiting for Harlan to vote on bifurcation, Fortas resigned from the Court. If Harlan had joined the opinion of the remaining four, the death penalty in Arkansas would have been struck down—at least until bifurcated trials were written into law. But Harlan did not do so, and the Court lacked a majority vote on any issue in *Maxwell*. It scheduled the case to be argued for a second time the following term, in 1970.

Before *Maxwell* was reargued, the makeup of the Court changed again. Fortas's place remained empty; Harry Blackmun would later fill it. First, though, Warren retired. He was replaced as chief justice by Warren Burger, who did not share Warren's opinion that the lack of a bifurcated trial was unconstitutional. The majority had evaporated, although the Court did agree that jury selection in Maxwell's trial had failed to meet the *Witherspoon* standard—several prospective jurors were rejected after they expressed scruples about the death penalty. The Court vacated Maxwell's sentence and returned the case to a lower court for retrial. Yet if it had not undergone two personnel shifts, it would have found the Arkansas death penalty laws unconstitutional, and the LDF would have won a significant victory.

Jury discretion and bifurcated trials did not go away. The LDF had pressed those points in *amicus curiae* briefs for other appeals besides *Maxwell*. In 1971 the Supreme Court heard two of those appeals, *Crampton* v. *Ohio* and *McGautha* v. *California*, combining them into a single case referred to as *McGautha*.

The petitioners in *McGautha* challenged unguided jury discretion on the grounds that it let juries apply the death penalty in a willy-nilly, inconsistent fashion, for any reason or for no reason at all. This violated the Fourteenth

Amendment guarantee of due process and equal protection. As far as bifurcation was concerned, Crampton had received both verdict and sentence in a single trial, while McGautha had received a two-stage trial. Crampton's representatives argued that defendants with bifurcated trials had advantages that others did not. The difference between the two systems was a violation of Crampton's due-process rights.

In conference with the other justices after the arguments in the case had been presented, Chief Justice Burger cut to the heart of the matter. Scornful of the notion of a bifurcated trial, Burger saw that the real target in *McGautha* was the death penalty itself. "This is an oblique attack on capital punishment . . . [the] abolition of capital punishment is what the case is all about."

The outcome of *McGautha* was discouraging to the LDF and other opponents of the death penalty. Douglas, Brennan, and Marshall thought that unguided jury discretion and the lack of a bifurcated trial were unconstitutional, but they were outvoted. Six justices came down firmly against guidelines for juries and two-part trials. As legal historian Stuart Banner notes, "The movement to use the courts to abolish capital punishment seemed to have come to an end."

Yet on June 28, 1971, about a month after issuing its decision in *McGautha*, the Supreme Court agreed to hear another batch of death-penalty cases, appeals that revolved around the Eighth Amendment ban on cruel and unusual punishments as well as the Fourteenth Amendment and due process. Did this mean that there might be hope after all for opponents of the death penalty? The thoughts of William Henry Furman, sitting on Death Row, were not recorded. Almost two years earlier, the state supreme court of Georgia had rejected his appeal. Now his case was on its way to the Supreme Court.

FIVE

FURMAN V. GEORGIA REACHES THE SUPREME COURT

IT WENT DOWN IN HISTORY as *Furman v. Georgia*, but the Supreme Court case that temporarily ended the death penalty was actually a combination of appeals against three different death sentences on constitutional grounds. The Supreme Court had consolidated them in order to hear and decide them at once.

Furman was one case. The other two were *Jackson v. Georgia* and *Branch v. Texas*. They concerned men who had been convicted of rape. Like Furman, Jackson and Branch had received death sentences. The Court had voted to grant *certiorari* to all three cases—to hear them, in other words—on a limited basis. It would accept arguments on just one question: "Does the imposition and carrying out of the death penalty in [these cases] constitute cruel and unusual punishment in violation of the Eighth and Fourteenth Amendments?" Everyone knew, though, that the significance of the Court's ruling would reach far beyond the death sentences of three men. If the Court overturned their sentences, many other death sentences would be overturned as well.

Preparations and Friends of the Court
The cases had been granted *certiorari* on the basis of briefs from the petitioners and respondents in all three cases.

These briefs summarized the main reasons why the Supreme Court should, or should not, hear each case. Once *Furman* had been placed on the Court's calendar, the attorneys for each side in each case prepared longer, more detailed briefs for the justices.

Briefs are extremely important in Supreme Court cases. They are the attorneys' opportunity to develop all of their arguments in detail and to provide whatever supporting evidence they intend to place before the Court.

JACK GREENBERG, HEAD OF THE NAACP AT THE TIME OF THE *FURMAN* CASE, REPRESENTED BOTH WILLIAM HENRY FURMAN AND LUCIOUS JACKSON BEFORE THE SUPREME COURT.

Furman would be heard by the justices in open court on January 17, 1972. At that time, however, each side would be limited to brief oral arguments, in which they would have to sum up their positions as concisely up possible, as well as answer any questions put to them by the justices. The real chance to get their points across to the justices came before that time, through the briefs.

Amicus curiae briefs may also be submitted to the Supreme Court while it is getting ready to hear a case. In *Furman*, the Court received eight such briefs. One of them, from the Indiana attorney general's office, urged the Court to affirm, or uphold, the death sentences that had been given in the lower courts. The other seven *amicus* briefs urged the Court to reverse, or overturn, the death sentences. These briefs came from the state of Alaska; the National Association for the Advancement of Colored People (NAACP); the American Civil Liberties Union (ACLU); the Synagogue Council of America; the West Virginia Council of Churches; James V. Bennett, a former director of prisons for the Department of Justice; and Edmund G. Brown, a former governor of California (he had been governor at the time of the controversial Caryl Chessman execution).

Petitioners and Respondents

Two of the petitioners, William Henry Furman and Lucious Jackson, were represented by lawyers from the NAACP's Legal Defense and Educational Fund (LDF). In Furman's case, Anthony Amsterdam was the lead attorney and would argue the case before the Supreme Court justices. Also representing Furman were his original attorney, B. Clarence Mayfield, and five members of the LDF: Michael Meltsner, Jack Greenberg, James M. Nabrit III, Jack Himmelstein, and Elizabeth B. DuBois. The same six LDF lawyers represented Jackson, with Greenberg as the lead attorney. The third petitioner, Elmer Branch, was represented by Melvyn C. Bruder, who was not associated with the LDF.

The petitioners' central arguments were written by the LDF attorneys. They addressed the Eighth Amendment issue by claiming that the death penalty was a "cruel and unusual" punishment. Capital punishment had not always been cruel and unusual, they admitted—but it must be seen that way in the 1970s. A survey of the history of capital punishment showed that its use and acceptability were decreasing. By the "evolving standards of decency" that the Court had acknowledged in *Trop* (1958), the death penalty had outlived its time. Pointing out that many nations had abolished or were abolishing capital punishment, the LDF wrote, "Like flogging and banishment, capital punishment is condemned by history and will sooner or later be condemned by this Court under the Constitution. The question is whether that condemnation should come sooner or later."

To support his claim that the death penalty was obsolete and cruel, Amsterdam offered an unusual argument. The public accepted capital punishment, he claimed, only because executions were so rare. Although more than fifteen thousand murders took place in the United States each year, only about a hundred murderers each year received death sentences, and fewer still were actually executed. If *all* death sentences were carried out, however, the public would reject the death penalty as unacceptably bloodthirsty.

The LDF also addressed the Fourteenth Amendment on the grounds that the death penalty was applied inconsistently and arbitrarily. Without a reasoned, consistent basis for applying the death penalty, defendants' due process and equal protection rights were violated. Arguing for Furman, Amsterdam pointed out that under the current system, in which some juries received sentencing guidelines while others did not, and some defendants received separate sentencing hearings while others did not, a cold-blooded killer who tortured and murdered multiple victims could receive life in prison, while Furman, who had shot a man without even knowing where his gun was pointed, got the death penalty.

Jack Greenberg, representing convicted rapist Jackson, also introduced the issue that had originally brought the LDF into death-penalty lawsuits: racial discrimination. In addition to arguing that death was an excessive penalty for a rapist who had not killed, Greenberg claimed that the use of the death penalty in rape cases violated the Fourteenth Amendment because blacks were more likely to receive death sentences than whites. Amsterdam made the same claim about executions for murder.

The respondents in the case were the states of Georgia and Texas. Dorothy T. Beasley, Georgia's assistant attorney general, was the lead attorney in *Furman* and *Jackson*, with support from the attorney general and other members of Georgia's legal department. Attorney Charles Alan Wright, representing Texas, was joined in that brief by the state's attorney general and others.

The states' attorneys mustered a variety of arguments in favor of upholding the three men's death sentences. They reminded the justices that the death penalty is specifically mentioned, but not prohibited, in the Fifth, Eighth, and Fourteenth Amendments to the Constitution. Not only was capital punishment accepted as part of the criminal system when the nation was founded, but it could not be considered cruel and unusual by contemporary American standards because it was part of the law code in forty of the fifty states.

The respondents' attorneys also pointed out that it was

not the place of the Supreme Court to make new laws but to interpret existing ones, arguing that if public opinion were truly against the death penalty, Congress and the state legislatures would recognize that fact with changes to the laws. The attorneys denied that the evidence showed any intentional or systematic discrimination in the use of the death penalty, and they stated that the issues of jury discretion and separate sentencing hearings had been settled in the *McGautha* case the previous year.

The oral arguments in *Furman* were uneventful. Neither the petitioners' nor the respondents' attorneys introduced any new elements or arguments. The drama came four days later, when the justices met for their first and only face-to-face conference on the case. Among them were two new justices who had taken their seats on the Supreme Court shortly before *Furman* was heard. The Court had changed a lot since *Maxwell* v. *Bishop*, just three years earlier, when it had come close to declaring the Arkansas death penalty unconstitutional.

ATTORNEY ALAN WRIGHT LED THE CASE FOR TEXAS AGAINST FURMAN. WRIGHT SOON JOINED THE WHITE HOUSE AS LEGAL COUNSEL DURING THE NIXON ADMINISTRATION.

THE CHANGING COURT

Justices of the Supreme Court are appointed by presidents, and they remain in their positions until they resign or die. A justice's term of service—and his or her influence on how the Constitution is interpreted—may span decades. Yet as the personnel of the Court changes over time, its overall stance on political and social issues shifts, too.

Presidents tend to appoint justices who belong to their political parties and share their general views. Since the mid-twentieth century, for example, the justices appointed by Republican presidents have been generally conservative, in favor of established institutions and reluctant to engineer social change by law. Those appointed by Democrats have been generally liberal, favoring individual rights and government action to encourage social change. But there are always exceptions. Earl Warren was a Republican governor of California before Republican President Dwight D. Eisenhower appointed him to the Court in 1953. To the surprise and displeasure of Eisenhower, Warren proved to be a liberal chief justice at the head of a liberal Court.

The Warren Court strengthened civil rights with decisions such as *Brown* v. *Board of Education* and *Miranda* v. *Arizona*. The makeup of the Court began to change, however, when Abe Fortas, a very liberal justice, resigned in 1969. Earl Warren's own resignation for health reasons came a month later. Richard M. Nixon, a Republican, was president at the time. He replaced Warren with a new chief justice, Warren Burger, and replaced Fortas with Harry Blackmun. Both were conservatives who interpreted the Constitution narrowly, or strictly.

By the time *Furman* came before the Court, two more justices had resigned. Two Nixon appointees took their places in January 1972: William H. Rehnquist replaced John Harlan, and Lewis Powell filled Hugo Black's seat. The Warren Court was giving way to the more conservative Burger Court—but five members of the Warren Court remained.

On January 21, 1972, the nine justices met to discuss *Furman*. In keeping with Supreme Court practice, they held a preliminary vote to see where everyone stood. Burger, as chief justice, spoke first. While acknowledging that "[a]ll of us have reservations about the death penalty," he was in favor of upholding the death sentences.

The rest of the justices would speak in order of their seniority on the Court. This meant that the other three new justices, Blackmun, Rehnquist, and Powell, would be last. As Nixon appointees, they could be expected to vote for the death penalty, as Burger had done. First, though, the remaining five justices had to cast their votes. If even one of them voted to uphold the death sentences, capital punishment would be supported by a 5 to 4 majority.

William O. Douglas had already revealed some uneasiness about jury discretion in *Maxwell* and *McGautha*. He now said that Anthony Amsterdam's argument about racial discrimination in the application of the death penalty disturbed him. Douglas came down against the death sentences. So did William Brennan, as expected. Brennan, who held the view that the Court could drive social change, had long been recognized as an opponent of capital punishment.

Potter Stewart came next. Even though Stewart had written the majority opinion that did away with "hanging juries" in *Witherspoon*, he had rejected broad constitutional attacks on capital punishment. No one expected him to find the death sentences in *Furman* unconstitutional. He said, however, that he did find them unconstitutional—tentatively. He was still thinking it over, but he didn't like the idea that if two people committed very similar crimes, one might receive death while the other went to prison.

Byron White had opposed *Miranda*, *Witherspoon*, and other decisions that enlarged criminals' and defendants' civil rights. He had no sympathy for the view that the Supreme Court should lead society in new directions. Yet

THE MEMBERS OF THE COURT AT THE TIME OF THE *FURMAN* CASE: *FRONT ROW*
(*L TO R*): ASSOCIATE JUSTICES POTTER STEWART, WILLIAM O. DOUGLAS, CHIEF
JUSTICE WARREN BURGER, ASSOCIATE JUSTICES WILLIAM J. BRENNAN JR. AND
BYRON R. WHITE. *BACK* (*L TO R*): ASSOCIATE JUSTICES LEWIS POWELL JR.,
THURGOOD MARSHALL, HARRY BLACKMUN, AND WILLIAM H. REHNQUIST.

like Stewart, White was bothered by inconsistencies in the
way the death penalty was applied. "The nub of the case,"
he said, "is that only a small proportion [of those con-
victed] are put to death." He was inclined to find the death

THrouGH THe courT sysTem

First Stop: State Court
Almost all cases (about 95 percent) start in state courts. These courts go by various names, depending on the state in which they operate: circuit, district, municipal, county, or superior. The case is tried and decided by a judge, a panel of judges, or a jury.

The side that loses can then appeal to the next level.

First Stop: Federal Court
U.S. DISTRICT COURT—About 5 percent of cases begin their journey in federal court. Most of these cases concern federal laws, the U.S. Constitution, or disputes that involve two or more states. They are heard in one of the ninety-four U.S. district courts in the nation.

U.S. COURT OF INTERNATIONAL TRADE—Federal court cases involving international trade appear in the U.S. Court of International Trade.

U.S. COURT OF FEDERAL CLAIMS—The U.S. Court of Federal Claims hears federal cases that involve more than $10,000, Indian claims, and some disputes with government contractors.

The loser in federal court can appeal to the next level.

Appeals: State Cases
Forty states have appeals courts that hear cases that have come from the state courts. In states without an appeals court, the case goes directly to the state supreme court.

Appeals: Federal Cases
U.S. CIRCUIT COURT—Cases appealed from U.S. district courts go to U.S. circuit courts of appeals. There are twelve circuit courts that handle cases from throughout the nation. Each district court and every state and territory

are assigned to one of the twelve circuits. Appeals in a few state cases—those that deal with rights guaranteed by the U.S. Constitution—are also heard in this court.

U.S. COURT OF APPEALS—Cases appealed from the U.S. Court of International Trade and the U.S. Court of Federal Claims are heard by the U.S. Court of Appeals for the Federal Circuit. Among the cases heard in this court are those involving patents and minor claims against the federal government.

Further Appeals: State Supreme Court
Cases appealed from state appeals courts go to the highest courts in the state—usually called supreme courts. In New York, the state's highest court is called the court of appeals. Most state cases do not go beyond this point.

Final Appeals: U.S. Supreme Court
The U.S. Supreme Court is the highest court in the country. Its decision on a case is the final word. The Court decides issues that can affect every person in the nation. It has decided cases on slavery, abortion, school segregation, and many other important issues.

The Court selects the cases it will hear—usually around one hundred each year. Four of the nine justices must vote to consider a case in order for it to be heard. Almost all cases have been appealed from the lower courts (either state or federal).

Most people seeking a decision from the Court submit a petition for *certiorari*. *Certiorari* means that the case will be moved from a lower court to a higher court for review. The Court receives about nine thousand of these requests annually. The petition outlines the case and gives reasons why the Court should review it.

In rare cases, for example *New York Times* v. *United States*, an issue must be decided immediately. When such a case is of national importance, the Court allows it to bypass the usual lower court system and hears the case directly.

To win a spot on the Court's docket, a case must fall within one of the following categories:

· Disputes between states and the federal government or between two or more states. The Court also reviews cases involving ambassadors, consuls, and foreign ministers.

· Appeals from state courts that have ruled on a federal question.

· Appeals from federal appeals courts (about two-thirds of all requests fall into this category).

sentences unconstitutional. Next came Thurgood Marshall. To no one's surprise, Marshall, the former civil-rights activist, voted to overturn the death sentences.

Something momentous was happening. Five justices—a majority—had indicated that they thought the death penalty was, or at least might be, unconstitutional. If they held to that position after full consideration and debate of the case, the Court would issue one of the most important, and controversial, decisions in its history.

Nothing was definite yet, however. For one thing, the conference had made it clear that the five justices who wanted to overturn the sentences in *Furman* had differing reasons for their decisions. Their views on some questions raised in the briefs varied sharply. For another thing, both Stewart and White had said that their votes were tentative; they might yet change their minds. As a result, the justices agreed that each of them would write his own opinion in the case.

Nine Justices, Nine Opinions

On June 29, 1972, the Supreme Court announced its decision in *Furman* v. *Georgia*. More than five months had passed since the conference, but the positions of the nine justices had not changed. A majority of sorts existed, in the sense that five of the nine had voted to reverse the death sentences, but each justice had a unique response to the case.

The Court's rulings are usually presented in the form of a majority opinion that is written by one justice and signed by the others who concur, or agree. Justices who dissent from the majority opinion, and also those who concur, may write opinions of their own in order to place their thoughts on the case in the record. In *Furman*, however, each of the nine justices published an opinion on the case. Even the basic 5 to 4 decision to overturn the death sentences was not expressed in a majority opinion. Instead, the Court did something that it rarely does. It issued its decision *per curiam*, which is Latin for "by the court," in the form of a short, unsigned opinion. Although a decision *per curiam* has the force of law, it is less emphatic, and weaker as a precedent in later cases, than a signed decision, because a *per curiam* decision is a sign that the Court was profoundly divided in the way it arrived at its ruling.

The *Furman* decision was summed up in a sentence: "Imposition and carrying out of death penalty in these cases held to constitute cruel and unusual punishment in violation of Eighth and Fourteenth Amendments." The official report of the case, however, was anything but short. In fact, at 233 pages, it was the longest case report that the Supreme Court had ever issued. Some of the nine opinions were long and heavily footnoted with supporting texts. Still, the essence of each justice's views was clear.

Five justices called for the reversal of the death sentences in *Furman* on the grounds that they had violated the Eighth and Fourteenth Amendments. This had the effect of making the death penalty unconstitutional—but the full picture was more complicated than that.

Justice Thurgood Marshall.

Justice Marshall was one of two justices who had hoped for a sweeping abolition of the death penalty itself, in all circumstances. In his opinion, he examined the question of whether the death penalty served a useful purpose that could not be met by a lesser punishment. His review of the evidence suggested that capital punishment did not lower the murder rate, so deterrence was not a useful purpose. If the purpose of the death penalty was to encourage confessions or guilty pleas, such a purpose was unconstitutional. Capital punishment served no economic purpose, either. The appeals process in capital cases cost society as much as maintaining criminals in prison for life. As for retribution, Marshall argued that payback was an inappropriate goal—indeed, the Eighth Amendment's ban on cruel and unusual punishments was meant "to prevent punishment from becoming synonymous with vengeance."

Marshall summed up his position this way: "There is but one conclusion that can be drawn from all this—i.e., the death penalty is an excessive and unnecessary punishment that violates the Eighth Amendment." Abolishing capital punishment, he declared, was a step on the road from barbarism to civilization.

Justice William Brennan Jr.

Justice Brennan agreed with Marshall that the death penalty itself was a cruel and unusual punishment, and thus flatly unconstitutional. He reached that conclusion, however, by a different route. Brennan argued that capital punishment was contrary to "the dignity of man" that had been held up as a standard in the 1958 *Trop* decision. In his view, death was an outmoded form of punishment, one that was being left behind by the "evolving standards of decency" of which Chief Justice Earl Warren had written in *Trop*. Society, Brennan argued, was moving away from acceptance of the death penalty—this was clear from the fact that it was performing fewer and fewer executions. True, the majority of states still authorized the death penalty, and polls showed that a sizable percentage of the American public supported it, but actions speak louder than words, and what really mattered was the declining execution rate. After arguing that the death penalty was arbitrarily applied and also ineffective as a deterrent to crime, Brennan said, "Death is today a 'cruel and unusual' punishment."

Justice William O. Douglas.

Justice Douglas agreed with Marshall and Brennan that the death sentences in *Furman* should be overturned, but he did not agree with them that the death penalty was unconstitutional in any circumstances. Douglas's opinion came to be seen as the essential meaning of the *Furman* ruling: The death penalty was unconstitutional *as it was being applied*. The problem was not with capital punishment itself but with the way it was handed out.

Douglas found that the death penalty as applied in the *Furman* cases (and, by extension, in all capital cases that had been decided under similar sentencing laws—which meant all Death-Row cases in the country at the time) was not just arbitrary and inconsistent but also racially discriminatory. Pointing out that all three petitioners were African-American, Douglas wrote:

> We cannot say from facts disclosed in these records that these defendants were sentenced to death because they were black. Yet our task is not restricted to an effort to divine what motives impelled these death penalties. Rather, we deal with a system of law and of justice that leaves to the uncontrolled discretion of judges or juries the determination whether defendants committing these crimes should die or be imprisoned. Under these laws no standards govern the selection of the penalty. People live or die, dependent on the whim of one man or of 12.

The current death-penalty laws did not *mean* to favor white defendants over black ones, or rich people over poor. If the laws indirectly favored certain groups over others, however, the effect was the same. The solution would be to introduce sentencing guidelines to make the application of the death penalty more fair, consistent, and rational.

Justice Byron White.

Justice White's opinion had the same effect as Douglas's: the current application of the death-penalty laws was unconstitutional, but that could be remedied. White wrote, "I do not at all intimate [suggest] that the death penalty is unconstitutional per se or that there is no system of capital punishment that would comport with the Eighth Amendment."

In White's view, there was nothing to prevent society from considering death an appropriate punishment for murder or rape, or from feeling that "those executed may deserve exactly what they received." Recognizing also the argument that the death penalty was a deterrent against other crime, White accepted "the morality and utility of punishing one person to influence another." Yet the death penalty was so seldom carried out that it had ceased to be effective as a deterrent: "I cannot avoid the conclusion that as the statutes before us are now administered, the penalty is so infrequently imposed that the threat of execution is too attenuated to be of substantial service to criminal justice," White wrote, implying that one way to make the death penalty constitutional would be to hold more executions. White claimed that the arbitrary, inconsistent nature of the death penalty was caused by the lack of a systematic legal framework for ensuring consistent sentences:

> The short of it is that the policy of vesting sentencing authority primarily in juries—a decision largely motivated by the desire to mitigate the harshness of the law and to bring community judgment to bear on the sentence as well as guilt or innocence—has so effectively achieved its aims that capital punishment within the confines of the

statutes now before us has for all practical purposes run its course.

Because the death penalty did not serve any useful purpose as it was currently being applied, it must be considered a cruel and unusual punishment—a violation of the Eighth Amendment.

Justice Potter Stewart.

Justice Stewart launched his opinion with a powerful statement of the great seriousness of capital punishment:

> The penalty of death differs from all other forms of criminal punishment, not in degree but in kind. It is unique in its total irrevocability. It is unique in its rejection of rehabilitation of the convict as a basic purpose of criminal justice. And it is unique, finally, in its absolute renunciation of all that is embodied in our concept of humanity.

Retribution, Stewart declared, has its place as one purpose of punishment:

> The instinct for retribution is part of the nature of man, and channeling that instinct in the administration of criminal justice serves an important purpose in promoting the stability of a society governed by law. When people begin to believe that organized society is unwilling or unable to impose upon criminal offenders the punishment they "deserve," then there are sown the seeds of anarchy—of self-help, vigilante justice, and lynch law.

After these philosophical points, however, Stewart

defined his approach to *Furman* very narrowly. His obligation to rule on the constitutionality of the death sentences in the case did not require him to rule on the status of capital punishment in the abstract. Stewart concluded that the death sentences in question were unconstitutional for the same reason advanced by White—the random, arbitrary nature of the sentencing process. He wrote:

> These death sentences are cruel and unusual in the same way that being struck by lightning is cruel and unusual. For, of all the people convicted of rapes and murders in 1967 and 1968, many just as reprehensible as these, the petitioners are among a capriciously selected random handful upon whom the sentence of death has in fact been imposed. My concurring Brothers have demonstrated that, if any basis can be discerned for the selection of these few to be sentenced to die, it is the constitutionally impermissible basis of race.... But racial discrimination has not been proved, and I put it to one side. I simply conclude that the Eighth and Fourteenth Amendments cannot tolerate the infliction of a sentence of death under legal systems that permit this unique penalty to be so wantonly and so freakishly imposed.

Chief Justice Warren Burger.
Chief Justice Burger wrote a dissent in which he presented his reasons for thinking that the petitioners' death sentences should not be reversed. It also expressed his views on the broader question of the constitutionality of capital punishment in general and the role of the Court. Justices Blackmun, Powell, and Rehnquist added their names to his dissent.

Although Burger expressed the personal opinion that capital punishment should be reserved for "a small category of the most heinous crimes," he added that the Court's proper business, constitutional inquiry, must be separated from personal feeling. The death penalty, Burger said, did not violate either the Eighth or the Fourteenth Amendment. Not only was capital punishment recognized in the Constitution, but it remained acceptable to the American public. "There are no obvious indications that capital punishment offends the conscience of society to such a degree that our traditional deference to the legislative judgment must be abandoned," wrote Burger. He meant that it had traditionally been the business of the legislatures, not the courts, to authorize or prohibit capital punishment, reflecting the will of the people, and it should remain so. "In a democracy the legislative judgment is presumed to embody the basic standards of decency prevailing in the society."

Burger also rejected the argument that juries acted arbitrarily and discriminatorily in sentencing some, but not all, capital defendants to death. He wrote:

It is argued that in those capital cases where juries have recommended mercy, they have given expression to civilized values and effectively renounced the legislative authorization for capital punishment. At the same time it is argued that where juries have made the awesome decision to send men to their deaths, they have acted arbitrarily and without sensitivity to prevailing standards of decency. This explanation for the infrequency of imposition of capital punishment is unsupported by known facts, and is inconsistent in principle with everything this Court has ever said about the functioning of juries in capital cases.

One aspect of Burger's opinion had considerable significance for the future of the death penalty after *Furman.*
Burger noted that legislatures could write new death-
penalty laws that the Court would accept. One approach
would be to provide sentencing standards; another would
be to limit the list of capital crimes. What was necessary
was to avoid applying the death penalty in "a random and
unpredictable manner."

Justice Lewis Powell Jr.

Justice Powell wrote a dissent that Burger, Rehnquist, and
Blackmun joined. He accepted that the concepts of "cruel
and unusual punishments" and "due process of law" were
not meant to remain forever enshrined in their original
meanings but to change over time as society's circumstances changed. Adaptability, however, did not mean a
complete change in meaning. Although it was permissible
to review specific cases for violations of the Eighth
Amendment, to abolish capital punishment completely
must be the concern of lawmakers, not the courts. Wrote
Powell:

> While flexibility in the application of these broad
> concepts is one of the hallmarks of our system of
> government, the Court is not free to read into the
> Constitution a meaning that is plainly at variance
> with its language. Both the language of the Fifth
> and Fourteenth Amendments and the history of
> the Eighth Amendment confirm beyond doubt
> that the death penalty was considered to be a con-
> stitutionally permissible punishment. It is, how-
> ever, within the historic process of constitutional
> adjudication to challenge the imposition of the
> death penalty in some barbaric manner or as a
> penalty wholly disproportionate to a particular

criminal act. And in making such a judgment in a case before it, a court may consider contemporary standards to the extent they are relevant. While this weighing of a punishment against the Eighth Amendment standard on a case-by-case basis is consonant with history and precedent, it is not what petitioners demand in these cases. They seek nothing less than the total abolition of capital punishment by judicial fiat.

As for the claim that the American public had come to find capital punishment unacceptable, Powell disagreed. He pointed out that the reversal of the death sentences "invalidates a staggering number of state and federal laws" by wiping out existing capital punishment statutes. In regard to the argument that the death penalty was unconstitutionally discriminatory, Powell wrote:

> Certainly the claim is justified that this criminal sanction [the death penalty] falls more heavily on the relatively impoverished and underprivileged elements of society. The "have-nots" in every society always have been subject to greater pressure to commit crimes and to fewer constraints than their more affluent fellow citizens. This is, indeed, a tragic byproduct of social and economic deprivation, but it is not an argument of constitutional proportions under the Eighth or Fourteenth Amendment. The same discriminatory impact argument could be made with equal force and logic with respect to those sentenced to prison terms.

If the Court accepted the argument that the death penalty was discriminatory, Powell argued, it would have to extend the same argument to every other kind of punishment, which would mean that society could not have a workable justice system.

Justice William Rehnquist.

Justice Rehnquist's dissenting opinion was signed by Burger, Powell, and Blackmun. Rehnquist focused on the role of the Supreme Court as it had been defined by the Founding Fathers. That role, he insisted, was to interpret laws strictly, not so broadly that interpretation became another form of lawmaking. In voting to reverse the *Furman* death sentences, and thereby ending capital punishment as it was practiced in every state, the Court had acted outside its proper role:

> Whatever its precise rationale, today's holding [decision] necessarily brings into sharp relief the fundamental question of the role of judicial review in a democratic society. How can government by the elected representatives of the people co-exist with the power of the federal judiciary, whose members are constitutionally insulated from responsiveness to the popular will, to declare invalid laws duly enacted by the popular branches of government? . . . I conclude that this decision holding unconstitutional capital punishment is not an act of judgment, but rather an act of will.

Justice Harry Blackmun.

In addition to joining Burger's, Powell's, and Rehnquist's dissents, Justice Blackmun wrote one of his own. His views were primarily personal. "Cases such as these provide for me an excruciating agony of the spirit," Blackmun began. "I yield to no one in the depth of my distaste, antipathy, and, indeed, abhorrence, for the death penalty, with all its aspects of physical distress and fear and of moral judgment exercised by finite minds. That distaste is buttressed by a belief that capital punishment serves no useful purpose that can be demonstrated."

If he were a legislator, Blackmun said, he would work to abolish capital punishment, but as a justice of the Supreme Court, he must limit himself to strict interpretation of the Constitution. In reversing the death sentences in *Furman*, the Court had crossed the line between interpreting the Constitution and seeking to achieve a goal. Blackmun concluded, "Although personally I may rejoice at the Court's result, I find it difficult to accept or to justify as a matter of history, of law, or of constitutional pronouncement. I fear the Court has overstepped. It has sought and has achieved an end."

But what end, or outcome, had the Court achieved?

SIX
THE DEATH PENALTY
AFTER FURMAN

DEATH ROW prisoners weren't the only people celebrating on June 29, 1972, the day the Supreme Court announced its ruling in *Furman* v. *Georgia*. The lawyers of the Legal Defense and Educational Fund (LDF) partied in their office, and death-penalty opponents everywhere rejoiced that a milestone had been reached. In reversing the death sentences of three men who had been condemned under the laws of two states, the Court had effectively struck down every death-penalty law in the nation.

Yet the Court's decision had been anything but unanimous. Four dissenting justices had supported the death penalty laws. Of the five who had concurred in the decision to reverse the sentences, just two had held that the death penalty itself was unconstitutional. The other three had found fault only with the laws that governed the application of the death penalty. And the opinions of justices on both the dissenting and concurring sides had suggested or implied ways to remedy the shortcomings of those laws. At the very moment *Furman* struck down the death penalty, it also showed the way for its resurrection.

THE DEATH PENALTY RETURNS
The fractured nature of the *Furman* decision reflected deep divisions in American attitudes toward the death

penalty. Although several justices had claimed that society was moving away from support for capital punishment, only one poll, in 1966, had ever shown that more Americans opposed the death penalty than supported it. In November 1972, five months after the *Furman* decision, a Gallup poll found that 57 percent of Americans supported capital punishment and 32 percent opposed it. The "standards of decency" that were supposed to guide the interpretation of the Eighth Amendment's cruel and unusual punishments clause appeared to be evolving toward a return of the death penalty.

In fact, no sooner had *Furman* suspended capital punishment across the land than state legislatures began crafting new death-penalty laws that, they hoped, would stand up to constitutional scrutiny. It was, writes legal historian Stuart Banner, "the biggest flurry of capital punishment legislation the nation had ever seen."

Florida was the first state to reintroduce the death penalty, enacting its new law five months after the *Furman* decision. Within four years, another thirty-four states and the federal government also had new capital-punishment laws in place.

The new statutes took several approaches to ending the arbitrariness of sentencing. One of these approaches was mandatory sentencing, in which the law demanded the death penalty for certain crimes. This removed the troublesome inconsistency of jury discretion.

A second approach was to leave sentencing in the hands of juries, but to build into the law guidelines that would make their sentences more consistent. Many of the states that took this approach adopted elements of the Model Penal Code, a sample death-penalty law written by attorneys, judges, and law professors. The Model Penal Code called for separate proceedings for the verdict and the sentence—the "bifurcated trial" that the Supreme

Court had considered in *McGautha*. The code also identified eight aggravating factors and eight mitigating factors that juries would have to consider when deciding between death and imprisonment. Aggravating factors would tilt the jury's decision toward death; they included such things as earlier convictions for violent crimes or special cruelty toward victims. Mitigating factors, such as a convicted person's youth or clean criminal record, would tilt the decision toward imprisonment.

The states that adopted new sentencing procedures did not always follow the Model Penal Code exactly. Instead, they produced an array of sentencing guidelines for jurors. Georgia, for example, had ten aggravating factors and no mitigating factors.

Another Milestone

The revived death penalty came before the Supreme Court in early 1976. *Furman* had emptied Death Row, but since that time hundreds of people had been convicted and sentenced under the new laws. In 1975 alone, 298 people received the death sentence. No one was executed, however, because the new laws were immediately challenged by appeals in the state courts. Some of these appeals then moved on to the Supreme Court.

Of the many requests it received from petitioners, the Supreme Court agreed to hear *Woodson v. North Carolina*, whose petitioner had received the death sentence under North Carolina's mandatory sentencing law. It also agreed to hear several petitioners who had been sentenced under new state laws that incorporated "guided discretion," or sentencing guidelines for jurors. All of these cases were grouped together as *Gregg v. Georgia*.

As in *Furman*, the LDF took the central role in representing the petitioners in *Gregg*. Anthony Amsterdam was its lead attorney for the petitioners at the oral arguments.

On the other side, the states were represented by attorneys, but their most vocal spokesperson was the solicitor general of the United States, Robert Bork. He had written a long *amicus curiae* brief for the case, supporting the death-penalty laws on behalf of the federal government, and as a representative of the government he was permitted to give an oral argument.

As the Court reviewed the case, the states, the public, and the world wondered whether the newly restored death penalty would survive. On July 2, 1976, the Court put an end to speculation. Its ruling in *Gregg* was complicated, although less complicated than *Furman*. Four justices—Burger, Blackmun, Rehnquist, and White—voted to uphold all of the death-penalty laws. Two justices, Marshall and Brennan, stood by their earlier opinions in *Furman* that the death penalty was flatly unconstitutional. They voted to overturn all of the new laws. The remaining three justices—Stewart, Powell, and John Paul Stevens, who had replaced Douglas on the Court—voted to uphold some of the laws, but to overturn North Carolina's mandatory sentencing law.

With five votes against it, mandatory sentencing was out. Stewart, Powell, and Stevens agreed that while mandatory sentencing did remove the problem of jury inconsistency, it put juries in a straitjacket. It required jurors to choose the death penalty without letting them consider the defendant's character or past history as mitigating factors. In effect, mandatory sentencing removed the possibility of mercy from sentencing. Mandatory sentencing had another negative effect as well. That was jury nullification, which occurs when juries find defendants not guilty, regardless of the facts, in order to spare them from execution.

Although the Court had ruled out mandatory death sentences, it did not come close to imperiling the death penalty itself. Seven of the justices ruled that the new laws

THE *GREGG* DECISION, ONLY FOUR YEARS AFTER *FURMAN*, SIGNALED YET
ANOTHER SHIFT IN POPULAR OPINION IN THE UNITED STATES—THIS TIME, IN
FAVOR OF THE DEATH PENALTY. TROY LEON GREGG, TWENTY-THREE, WAS
CONVICTED OF KILLING TWO MEN AND SENTENCED TO DEATH.

of Georgia, Texas, and Florida were constitutional. All
three laws required separate sentencing hearings, but they
differed in various ways. Georgia's law demanded that at
least one aggravating factor be present for a death sentence. Under Florida's law, if an aggravating factor were
present, the jury was required to weigh mitigating evidence as well. The judge could override the jury's sentence, but only under strict and specific conditions. The
Texas law defined capital murder as a narrow category
apart from other homicides. Capital murder included the
killing of a police officer or firefighter who was on duty,

killing for hire, and deliberate killing during the course of another felony, such as rape or robbery. Someone convicted of capital murder could be sentenced to either death or life in prison; a series of questions guided the jurors as they made the decision.

As applied under these laws, the Court held, the death penalty did not violate defendants' due-process and equal-protection rights under the Fourteenth Amendment. Furthermore, as it had done in *Furman*, the Court rejected arguments that the death penalty was out of step with the "evolving standards of decency" of the time. It held that the death penalty was not a cruel and unusual punishment and did not violate the Eighth Amendment.

Gregg gave states the green light to implement the death penalty, as long as juries received adequate guidance. Half a year later, on January 17, 1977, the first execution in the United States since June 1967 took place. The condemned man was Gary Gilmore, convicted in Utah of murder. Like Wallace Wilkerson in the Utah Territory a century earlier, Gilmore was executed by firing squad—at his request.

THE COURT AND CAPITAL PUNISHMENT

The *Furman* and *Gregg* decisions were only four years apart, but they represent different eras in the history of American capital punishment. The movement to abolish the death penalty has always ebbed and flowed. So has public support for the death penalty. *Furman* came along soon after public support had reached its lowest point ever, at a time when the civil-rights movement and a somewhat liberal Court had created momentum for death-penalty abolition. But the aftermath of *Furman*, ironically, was a new wave of capital punishment laws that proved invulnerable to constitutional challenges in *Gregg*. Most states, and the American people in general, were clearly not ready to give up the death penalty.

Gregg, according to legal scholar Hugo Adam Bedau, "marked the defeat of the campaign to abolish the death penalty nationwide, all at once, and on constitutional grounds." It did not, however, mark the end of the Supreme Court's involvement in capital punishment. Since *Gregg*, the Court has ruled on dozens of death-penalty cases. Rather than attempting to overturn (or to uphold) capital punishment itself, these cases have focused on the ways the penalty is applied and administered. They have fine-tuned the constitutionality of the death sentence.

In 1976, for example, the same year as *Gregg*, the Court handed down its ruling in *Coker* v. *Georgia*, finding the death penalty unconstitutional as punishment for the rape of an adult. Ten years later, in *Ford* v. *Wainwright*, the Court ruled that it was unconstitutional to execute a condemned man who had become insane on Death Row; since that time, many cases have turned on questions of how mental illness is defined and how it affects death sentences. In 2002, in *Atkins* v. *Virginia*, the Court found it unconstitutional to apply the death penalty to mentally retarded defendants. Three years later, in *Roper* v. *Simmons*, it held that defendants who were under the age of eighteen when they committed their crimes could not be executed.

One of the most pressing death-penalty issues in the early years of the twenty-first century is the "innocence question." The fear of wrongful conviction and execution, of sentencing an innocent person to death, has haunted many people on both sides of the death-penalty debate. Advances in the science of using evidence, especially the genetic evidence of DNA, have played an increasing role in establishing guilt or innocence in cases where such evidence exists. The courts, along with defense attorneys and organizations such as the Innocence Project, have applied new tests to DNA collected in many cases over the years. Between 1993 and late 2006, DNA tests exonerated—

DNA ANALYSIS HAS PLAYED AN INCREASING ROLE IN DETERMINING GUILT OR INNOCENCE, AND HAS CAUSED OLD CASES TO BE REOPENED IN THE FACE OF NEW EVIDENCE.

proved the innocence—of more than a dozen Death Row inmates. Since 1973, more than a hundred others had been exonerated for other reasons, raising the disturbing possibility that innocent people may already have been executed.

The innocence question drove Illinois Governor George Ryan to commit the controversial act, in 2000, of suspending executions in his state. He was deeply troubled by the number of inmates—including Death Row inmates—who were being exonerated because of DNA tests or for other reasons. His duty to the people of his state, Ryan concluded, demanded that he halt capital punishment so that no one who was innocent would be executed. Three years later, just before his term as governor ended, Ryan commuted the sentences of all Death Row inmates in Illinois: 167 people. In a statement at the time, he asked, "How many more cases of wrongful conviction have to

WHAT HAPPENED AFTERWARD?

William Henry Furman's name was attached to one of the biggest Supreme Court cases of the twentieth century. The Court's decision reversed his death sentence and spared his life. What was Furman's life like after that?

A few months after the *Furman* decision, the Georgia Supreme Court converted Furman's sentence to life in prison. Twelve years later, in 1984, Furman was released on parole. Some years later, when interviewed by legal journalist Joan Cheever, Furman said that he had worked in construction but had given it up because of poor health. He claimed to have had two heart attacks. His record shows a series of arrests on alcohol and weapons-related charges.

In Macon, Georgia, Furman got into trouble with the law again. He was indicted on a charge of burglary in 2004, and again the following year. After the second charge he jumped bail, which is a felony in itself. In September 2006 the sixty-four-year-old Furman was arrested in Macon, charged with breaking into a woman's home. He was jailed without bond to await trial.

Furman's Supreme Court case had ended the death penalty and struck down Georgia's capital-punishment laws. Four years later, Troy Leon Gregg's case restored the death penalty.

Gregg had been convicted under Georgia's new capital statute of murdering two men who had given him and another man a ride when they were hitchhiking in 1973, a year after *Furman*. Three years later, the Supreme Court ruled in *Gregg* that the Georgia law was constitutional, and that Gregg's death sentence should stand. Gregg was not executed, though—at least, not by the state. He escaped from prison in 1980 while awaiting execution. The next night he was killed in a fight in a North Carolina bar.

occur before we can all agree that the system is broken?" The federal Innocence Protection Act, passed the following year, budgeted funds for programs to make DNA testing available to convicted inmates. In June 2006, in *House* v. *Bell*, the Supreme Court ruled that Paul House, who had been convicted of rape and murder in Tennessee in 1985, had the right to a retrial in federal court because DNA testing years after his conviction proved that biological material found on the victim had come from her husband, not from House.

As of early 2007, the death penalty was part of the law code for the U.S. government, the U.S. military, and every state except Alaska, Hawaii, Iowa, Maine, Massachusetts, Michigan, Minnesota, North Dakota, Rhode Island, Vermont, West Virginia, Wisconsin, and the District of Columbia. At the same time, many death-penalty states were shifting their positions on the issue. A few states were examining measures that could expand the death penalty. Missouri, for example, was considering a law that would make the death sentence mandatory for anyone who killed a law-enforcement officer, while Texas and Utah were considering extending the death penalty to certain sex crimes. If passed, such laws will no doubt be challenged on constitutional grounds before the Supreme Court.

Weakening the death penalty, or even eliminating it, is the goal of laws and policies being proposed in other states. In New Jersey, a state commission has recommended abolishing the death penalty. Bills to abolish the death penalty, or moratoriums to suspend it, had been introduced or proposed in ten other states by early 2007. Furthermore, following medical studies that suggested that lethal injection is far from painless, a number of states had suspended executions until questions about lethal injection were investigated and resolved. The result was that in some states the

THIRTY-THREE FORMER DEATH ROW INMATES SIT ON THE STAGE TOGETHER AS ANTHONY AMSTERDAM, THE LEAD LAWYER IN THE *FURMAN* CASE, SPEAKS AT A NATIONAL CONFERENCE ON WRONGFUL CONVICTIONS AND THE DEATH PENALTY AT NORTHWESTERN UNIVERSITY LAW SCHOOL IN CHICAGO ON NOVEMBER 14, 1998.

death penalty remained law but was no longer being carried out in practice. The number of people executed in 2006 was 53, a ten-year low. The number of death sentences has fallen, too. Throughout the 1990s judges and juries had sentenced about 300 people a year to death, but in 2006 only 114 people received the death sentence.

The early years of the twenty-first century may have seen the beginning of another shift in the American public's opinion on the death penalty. A Gallup poll in 2006 revealed that two-thirds of people still favored capital punishment for murderers. Yet when asked to choose which punishment they favored for convicted criminals— death or life imprisonment without parole—48 percent chose imprisonment, while 47 percent chose death. It was the first time in twenty years that more Americans had selected life in prison than execution as the appropriate punishment. At that time some members of the Supreme Court, including Chief Justice John Roberts, who joined the Court in 2005, and Justices Antonin Scalia and Samuel Alito, staunchly supported the death penalty. Still, if the

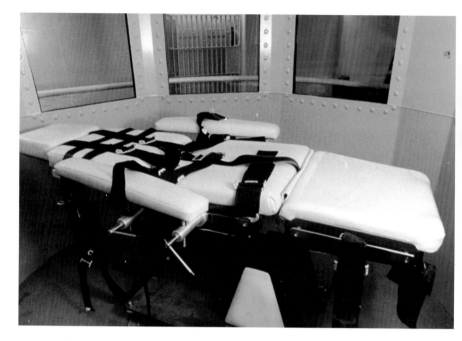

THIS PHOTO SHOWS A LETHAL INJECTION TABLE IN SAN QUENTIN PRISON. ONCE THOUGHT THE SAFEST, MOST EFFICIENT METHOD OF EXECUTION, LETHAL INJECTION IS NOW BEING QUESTIONED.

mood of the people were to shift away from support for capital punishment, as it has done in the past, changes in state laws could once again redraw the picture of the death penalty in America.

In classrooms and courtrooms, in print and on the Internet, in the United States and around the world, people are talking about the death penalty right now. Those who want to abolish capital punishment have arguments based on morality, religion, economics, statistics about crime and deterrence, polls, and visions of what is best for society. So do those who believe that the death penalty is right and necessary. Unlike murder victims, and the people who are executed for violent crimes, the debate lives on.

TImeLIne

1608   The first execution in the English colonies of America occurs in Jamestown, Virginia.

1689   The English Bill of Rights bans "cruel and unusual punishments."

1791   The Bill of Rights is added to the U.S. Constitution. Its Eighth Amendment copies the English ban on cruel and unusual punishments.

1797   Benjamin Rush publishes a pamphlet that launches the American movement to abolish the death penalty.

1846   Michigan abolishes capital punishment, becoming the first state to do so.

1878   The U.S. Supreme Court makes its first ruling on the Eighth Amendment in *Wilkerson v. Utah*.

1887   Maine abolishes the death penalty.

1890   The electric chair is used for the first time to execute William Kemmler in New York.

1910   Opinions in the Supreme Court case of *Weems v. United States* establish the principle that the definition of "cruel and unusual punishment" can change over time.

1907–   Capital punishment is abolished in nine states
1917   and Puerto Rico.

1918–   Four states that had abolished the death penalty
1921   restore it.

1950s Anti-death penalty feelings rise in the United States.

1967 Lawyers begin attacking the death penalty on constitutional grounds; William Henry Furman kills William Micke in Savannah, Georgia.

1968 A nationwide moratorium on executions begins; Furman is found guilty of murder and receives the death sentence.

1969 The Georgia Supreme Court upholds Furman's death sentence.

1971 The U.S. Supreme Court agrees to hear several cases on the constitutionality of the death penalty; one of them is *Furman*.

1972 The Supreme Court rules in *Furman* v. *Georgia* that existing death-penalty laws are unconstitutional; states begin rewriting capital-punishment laws.

1976 The Supreme Court rules in *Gregg* v. *Georgia* that the death penalty in itself is not unconstitutional.

1977 Gary Gilmore becomes the first person to be executed in the United States in ten years.

1986 The Supreme Court bans the execution of the insane in *Ford* v. *Wainwright*.

2000 Governor George Ryan of Illinois suspends capital punishment in his state; in 2003 he grants clemency to all Illinois Death Row inmates.

2002 The Supreme Court rules in *Atkins* v. *Virginia* that the execution of mentally retarded defendants is unconstitutional.

2005 The Supreme Court rules in *Roper* v. *Simmons* that the death penalty cannot be applied to offenders who were under eighteen when they committed their crimes.

notes

Chapter 1

p. 7, par. 1, Martin Waldron, "Ruling Cheered on
   Florida's Death Row," *New York Times*, June 30, 1972,
   14, and Stuart Banner, *The Death Penalty: An American
   History*, Cambridge, MA: Harvard University Press,
   2002.

p. 7, par. 3, Death Penalty Information Center,
   "Challenging the Death Penalty." http://www.death
   penaltyinfo.org/article.php?scid=15&did=410

p. 8, par. 2, Joan Cheever, "Finding Furman" in *Back
   from the Dead*, New York: Wiley, 2006,
   http://www.backfromthedeadusa.com/news_page
   7.html.

p. 10, par. 2, Brief for Petitioner, *Furman v. Georgia* in
   Philip B. Kurland and Gerhard Casper, eds.,
   Landmark Briefs and Arguments of the Supreme Court,
   Arlington, VA: University Publications of America,
   1975, 73:483.

p. 11, par. 1, American Civil Liberties Union ProCon.org
   case summary, http://www.acluprocon.org/
   SupCtCases/225Furman.html.

Chapter 2

p. 19, par. 1, Stuart Banner, *The Death Penalty: An
   American History*, Cambridge, MA: Harvard

University Press, 2002, 28.

p. 21, par. 2, Michael H. Reggio, "History of the Death Penalty," http://www.pbs.org/wgbh/pages/frontline/shows/execution/readings/history.html

p. 22, par. 3, Reggio, "History of the Death Penalty."

p. 24, par. 1, Quoted by Justice William O. Douglas in *Furman v. Georgia*, 408 U.S. 238, http://laws.findlaw.com/us/408/238.html

p. 26, par. 1, Banner, *The Death Penalty*, 7.

p. 26, par. 2, Quoted by Hugo Adam Bedau, "An Abolitionist's Survey of the Death Penalty in America," in Hugo Adam Bedau and Paul Cassell, eds., *Debating the Death Penalty*, New York: Oxford University Press, 2004, 15.

p. 26, par. 4, Reggio, "History of the Death Penalty."

p. 28, par. 3, Quoted by Douglas in *Furman v. Georgia*.

p. 29, par. 2, Cesare Beccaria, *An Essay on Crimes and Punishments*, quoted by Reggio, "History of the Death Penalty."

p. 31, par. 1, Banner, *The Death Penalty*, 99–100.

p. 31, par. 2, Banner, *The Death Penalty*, 98.

p. 34, par. 1, Bedau and Cassell, *Debating the Death Penalty*, 19.

p. 34, par. 2, Quoted in Banner, *The Death Penalty*, 29.

Chapter 3

p. 39, par. 2, *Wilkerson v. Utah*, 99 U.S. 130 (1878), http://laws.findlaw.com/us/99/130.html

p. 40, par. 2, Michael H. Reggio, "History of the Death Penalty," http://www.pbs.org/wgbh/pages/frontline/shows/execution/readings/history.html

p. 41, par. 3, Stuart Banner, *The Death Penalty: An American History*, Cambridge, MA: Harvard University Press, 2002, 178.

p. 41, par. 3, Ibid., 180.

p. 43, par. 1, *In re Kemmler*, 136 U.S. 436 (1890),
http://laws.findlaw.com/us/136/436.html

p. 43, par. 3, Banner, *The Death Penalty*, 186.

p. 45, par. 1, Banner, *The Death Penalty*, 185.

p. 48, par. 1, Justice Joseph McKenna in *Weems* v. *United
States*, 217 U.S. 349 (1910), http://laws.findlaw.com/
us/217/349.html

p. 48, par. 2, McKenna in *Weems* v. *United States*.

p. 51, par. 2, Justice Stanley F. Reed in *Francis* v. *Resweber*,
329 U.S. 459 (1947), http://laws.findlaw.com/
us/329/459.html

p. 51, par. 2, Reed in *Francis* v. *Resweber*.

p. 52, par. 2, Chief Justice Earl Warren in *Trop* v. *Dulles*,
356 U.S. 86 (1958), http://laws.findlaw. com/us/
356/86.html

Chapter 4

p. 54, par. 1, Hugo Adam Bedau, "An Abolitionist's
Survey of the Death Penalty in America," in Hugo
Adam Bedau and Paul Cassell, eds., *Debating the Death
Penalty*, New York: Oxford University Press, 2004, 22.

p. 54, par. 2, Death Penalty Information Center,
"Introduction to the Death Penalty: Early and Mid-
Twentieth Century," http://www.deathpenaltyinfo.
org/article.php?scid=15&did=410#poll

p. 54, par. 3, Stuart Banner, *The Death Penalty: An
American History*, Cambridge, MA: Harvard University
Press, 2002, 244.

p. 55, par. 1, Banner, *The Death Penalty*, 245.

p. 55, par. 2, Banner, *The Death Penalty*, 246–247.

p. 55, par. 3, Death Penalty Information Center,
"Introduction to the Death Penalty," and Banner, *The
Death Penalty*, 240.

p. 56, par. 1, Bedau and Cassell, *Debating the Death
Penalty*, 23.

p. 57, par. 1, Quoted by Justice Potter Stewart in *United States* v. *Jackson*, 390 U.S. 570 (1968), http://laws.findlaw.com/us/390/570.html

p. 60, par. 3, Justice Potter Stewart, *Witherspoon* v. *Illinois*, 391 U.S. 510 (1968), http://laws.findlaw.com/us/ 391/510.html

p. 60, par. 4, Quoted by Stewart, *Witherspoon* v. *Illinois*.

p. 61, par. 2, Stewart, *Witherspoon* v. *Illinois*.

p. 64, par. 5–p. 65, par. 1, Quoted in Stuart Banner in *The Death Penalty: An American History*, Cambridge, MA: Harvard University Press, 2002, 248.

p. 65, par. 2, Alan Dershowitz, *The Best Defense*, New York: Random House, 1982, 307.

p. 66, par. 1, Goldberg memorandum quoted in Banner, *The Death Penalty*, 249.

p. 68, par. 3, Banner, *The Death Penalty*, 250.

p. 69, par. 3, Milton Meltsner, *Cruel and Unusual: The Supreme Court and Capital Punishment*, New York: Random House, 1973, 107, cited in Banner, *The Death Penalty*, 252.

p. 76, par. 2–3, Banner, *The Death Penalty*, 257.

Chapter 5

p. 77, par. 2, *Furman* v. *Georgia*, 408 U.S. 238 (1972), http://laws.findlaw.com/us/408/238.html

p. 80, par. 2, Quoted in Stuart Banner, *The Death Penalty: An American History*, Cambridge, MA: Harvard University Press, 2002, 258–259.

p. 84, par. 1, Quoted in Banner, *The Death Penalty*, 260.

p. 85, par. 1, Quoted in Banner, *The Death Penalty*, 260–261.

p. 89, par. 2, , *Furman* v. *Georgia*.

p. 90, par. 2, Banner, *The Death Penalty*, 264.

p. 91, par. 1, *Furman* v. *Georgia*.

Chapter 6

p. 102, par. 2, Stuart Banner, *The Death Penalty: An American History*, Cambridge, MA: Harvard University Press, 2002, 267.

p. 102, par. 3, Death Penalty Information Center, Reinstating the Death Penalty, http://www.death penaltyinfo.org/article.php?scid=15&did=410

p. 102, par. 3, Banner, *The Death Penalty*, 268.

p. 103, par. 3, Banner, *The Death Penalty*, 270.

p. 106, par. 4, Hugo Adam Bedau, "An Abolitionist's Survey of the Death Penalty in America," in Hugo Adam Bedau and Paul Cassell, eds., *Debating the Death Penalty*, New York: Oxford University Press, 2004, 23.

p. 107, par. 3, Death Penalty Information Center, The Innocence List, http://www.deathpenaltyinfo.org/article.php?scid=6&did=110

p. 108, par. 1, George Ryan, "I Must Act," in Hugo Adam Bedau and Paul Cassell, eds., *Debating the Death Penalty*, New York: Oxford University Press, 2004, 222.

p. 109, par. 4, Tim Sturrock, "Man Behind Historic Death Penalty Case Back in Jail," *Macon Telegraph*, September 21, 2006, http://www.macon.com/mld/macon/15568709.htm

p. 109, par. 5, Jeffrey Anderson, "Inside the Tribe: Death Penalty Lawyers," *Daily Journal*, http://www.kupferer law.com/press/inside_the_tribe.html

p. 110, par. 3–p. 111, par. 1, Death Penalty Information Center, The Death Penalty in Flux, http://www.death penaltyinfo.org, and Death Penalty Fact Sheet, http://www.deathpenaltyinfo.org/factsheet.pdf

p. 111, par. 2, Dahlia Lithwick, "Sudden Death," slate.com, February 12, 2007, http://www.slate.com/id/2159373?nav=tap3

(All Web sites accessible as of March 16, 2007.)

FurTHer inFormaTion

Further Reading

Gottfried, Ted. *The Death Penalty: Justice or Legalized Murder?* Brookfield, CT: Twenty-First Century Books, 2002.

Henningfield, Diane Andrews, ed. *The Death Penalty: Opposing Viewpoints*. Farmington Hills, MI: Greenhaven, 2006.

Hines, Maurene J. *Furman v. Georgia and the Death Penalty Debate*. Berkeley Heights, NJ: Enslow, 2005.

LeVert, Suzanne. *The Supreme Court*. New York: Benchmark Books, 2002.

Patrick, John Jay. *The Supreme Court of the United States: A Student Companion*. New York: Oxford University Press Children's Books, 2002.

Steffens, Bradley. *Furman v. Georgia: Fairness and the Death Penalty*. San Diego, CA: Lucent, 2001.

Streissguth, Tom. *The Death Penalty: Debating Capital Punishment*. Berkeley Heights, NJ: Enslow, 2002.

Web Sites

American Civil Liberties Union Capital Punishment
http://www.aclu.org/capital/index.html

Cornell Death Penalty Project
http://library.lawschool.cornell.edu/death/

Criminal Justice Legal Foundation
  http://www.cjlf.org
Furman on FindLaw
  http://laws.findlaw.com/us/408/238.html
National Coalition to Abolish the Death Penalty
  http://www.ncadp.org
PBS History of the Death Penalty
  http://www.pbs.org/wgbh/pages/frontline/shows/
  execution/readings/history.html
Pro-Death-Penalty
  http://www.prodeathpenalty.com

(All Web sites accessible as of March 16, 2007.)

BIBLIOGraPHY

Books and Articles

Banner, Stuart. *The Death Penalty: An American History*. Cambridge, MA: Harvard University Press, 2002.

Bedau, Hugo, and Paul Cassell, eds. *Debating the Death Penalty*. New York: Oxford University Press, 2004.

Bessler, John D. *Kiss of Death: America's Love Affair with the Death Penalty*. Boston: Northeastern University Press, 2003.

Coyne, Randall. *Capital Punishment and the Judicial Process*. Durham, NC: Academic Press, 2001.

Foley, Michael A. *Arbitrary and Capricious: The Supreme Court, the Constitution, and the Death Penalty*. Westport, CT: Praeger, 2003.

Garvey, Stephen. *Beyond Repair? America's Death Penalty*. Durham, NC: Duke University Press, 2003.

Gershman, Gary P. *Death Penalty on Trial: A Handbook with Cases, Laws, and Documents*. Santa Barbara, CA: ABC-CLIO, 2005.

Latzer, Barry. *Death Penalty Cases: Leading U.S. Supreme Court Cases on Capital Punishment*. Boston: Butterworth-Heinemann, 2002.

Zimring, Franklin E. *The Contradictions of American Capital Punishment*. New York: Oxford University Press, 2003.

List of Cases Related to *Furman* v. *Georgia*

Wilkerson v. *Utah*, 99 U.S. 130 (1878)

Weems v. *United States*, 217 U.S. 349 (1910)

Louisiana ex re. Francis v. *Resweber*, 329 U.S. 459 (1947)

Trop v. *Dulles*, 356 U.S. 86 (1958)

United States v. *Jackson*, 390 U.S. 570 (1968)

Witherspoon v. *Illinois*, 391 U.S. 510 (1968)

McGautha v. *California*, 402 U.S. 183 (1971)

Furman v. *Georgia*, 408 U.S. 238 (1972)

Gregg v. *Georgia*, 428 U.S. 153 (1976)

Coker v. *Georgia*, 433 U.S. 584 (1977)

Tison v. *Arizona*, 482 U.S. 137 (1987)

Thompson v. *Oklahoma*, 487 U.S. 815 (1987)

Penry v. *Lynaugh*, 492 U.S. 302 (1989)

Atkins v. *Virginia*, 536 U.S. 304 (2002)

Ring v. *Arizona*, 536 U.S. 584 (2002)

Roper v. *Simmons*, 543 U.S. 551 (2005)

index

Page numbers in **boldface** are illustrations, tables, and charts.

about the author

REBECCA STEFOFF is the author of many nonfiction books for young adults, including *The Bakke Case: Challenging Affirmative Action* for the Supreme Court Milestones series. In addition to books on history, exploration, nature, and science, she has authored works on social history, writing about such topics as environmental activism and legislation, immigration, and Native American rights. Stefoff makes her home in Portland, Oregon. Information about her books for young people can be found at http://www.rebeccastefoff.com.